LIVING
GLOBALIZED

The Best Adventures are
Powered by International
Perspective

Commit to being a lifelong learner

Jeffrey Eker Jr.

Jeffrey Eker Jr.
&
Sarang Shaikh

CONTENTS

Introduction

This story is about two people who met in an elevator in Sri Lanka, who have before and since gained so much from traveling and working on the international level. Our journey starts with our paths crossing in that elevator in Sri Lanka at a very special conference hosted by a very special organization. Then, for the first half of the book, our narrative swings back in time to describe how we each individually grew on a personal and professional level before meeting in that elevator. We then pivot to "after the elevator" in the second half, where we describe the amazing opportunities we have received and lessons we have learned from our global work, travels, and volunteerism. The point? We live in a globalized economy, and for the first time have digital tools to connect with anyone around the globe at any time. Our book focuses on the fact that with a little hard work, anyone can leverage the opportunities made possible by our modern tools to actually travel, gain perspective, and make an impact at the global level.

I, Jeff, have now been to 22 countries, including: the United States (home), Canada (3x), Mexico, Costa Rica, Brazil (2x), Argentina, France (2x), Belgium, Luxembourg, Germany (5x), Austria, Switzerland, the United Arab Emirates, India (2x), Sri Lanka, China, Singapore, Indonesia (3x), Australia (2x), Iceland, Malaysia, and New Zealand.

I, Sarang, have now been to 12 countries including: Pakistan (home), USA (8x), UAE (6x), India, France, Netherlands, Czech Republic, Belgium, Qatar, Saudi Arabia, Sri Lanka, and Nepal.

The Institute of Electrical and Electronics Engineers (IEEE, pronounced "eye triple E") is the world's largest technical professional organization dedicated to advancing technology for the benefit of humanity. You'll see this acronym pop up a lot throughout our journeys, as it played a powerful role in facilitating them. Know that this is not an advertisement for the organization, just a description of our catalyst and one that you could replace with a myriad of other volunteer organizations, government programs, or corporate entities in your field of interest to make an impact on the global stage. Of course, we also have our moms and dads, two families on either side of the globe, to thank for supporting us and making everything you're about to read possible.

More than conveying our story, the goal of this book is help you develop your own journey in becoming a global citizen. As we share our stories and the lessons learned along the way, we have included some relevant action items at the end of each chapter that you can complete to learn just a little more about the world and further cement context around our growth journey captured in the chapter.

Capturing our travels from 2011 to January 1st, 2018, we put pen to paper to tell you our journey and how you, too, can follow in our footsteps. Whether you are in high school or university, a fresh entrepreneur, or a fledgling in the workforce – define your journey and follow a path of adventure that takes you down the road of utilizing, in every way possible, the technology and means of our modern, globalized ecosystem. Everyone who got where they are had to begin where they were. Welcome to Living Globalized!

Jeffrey Eker Jr. & Sarang Shaikh

1: THE ELEVATOR

Lesson: When things seem out of whack – especially when traveling internationally, serendipity is typically right around the corner.

It started with an emergency landing. My name is Jeff, and on this particular day, I found myself seemingly surgically embedded in my small middle-seat battlement on a United Airlines flight from Newark to Hong Kong; a new record for me at exactly 16 hours of flight time, or at least that was the plan. To my left was a CNN management-level staffer and to my right a former salesman from Japan.

It all began quite professionally with a brief announcement an hour after takeoff: "Ladies and gentlemen, there has been a main turbine failure. While we are still working with the airline management to determine the best course of action, standard procedure would have us dump fuel and return to Newark airport." While others around me shuffled uncomfortably in angst, my engineering mindset hardly had me batting an eyelash – these systems are triple redundant, after all. Presently, I was halfway into an engineering sales internship at 20 years old. The news that we would be turning back was devastating, however. More on that later; first, a backdrop.

Just before my senior year at Rowan University, pursuing an Electrical and Computer Engineering degree, I was on the first leg of an eight-day mission to quite literally fly all the way around the world. Wheels up from Boston to wheels back down in "the good ol' USA", I was headed from Boston to Singapore (including that Newark to Hong Kong connection), Singapore to Colombo, and straight back to Boston.

Two years prior I had begun my journey with the world's largest technical professional organization called IEEE. While we will get into the power-play of my initial involvement, I (along with most everyone in the organization) was astounded to learn that this professional society with approximately 400,000 members commands over $400 million dollars in revenue annually. IEEE had come to define much of my college success story while fueling my passion for working internationally. This trip was the to-date pinnacle of that passion. Just weeks earlier, I had learned that both the IEEE and the South Jersey Technology Park would indeed fund this fateful trip to an IEEE conference in Sri Lanka. The problem? My engineering sales internship had to be a minimum of 12 weeks, and I had no wiggle room to make it fit.

This internship had me traveling to manufacturing locations, analyzing automation at the plants, designing solutions to fill their design gaps, and conveying those solutions to customers. On a cool June morning in New England several weeks back, I found myself in Marlborough, Massachusetts at the local Rockwell Automation office. Fresh off the euphoria of receiving the funding to attend the conference in Sri Lanka, I sliced through the dense air, made musty by the gray fabric-covered cubes, to knock on the regional manager's office door. Throughout my first couple of weeks, I had learned that Don was incredible. He was levelheaded and loved winning. Winning was what the Boston territory did; we were good at it. Don turned my internship policy-driven brick wall of not being able to take time off during my internship into an opportunity. It turned out that an expert in serialization was needed to give a presentation to the Singapore Southeast Asia Headquarters, and an analysis of Rockwell's successful "Culture of Inclusion" program in North America was needed for its potential to expansion to the Asia offices. Don enabled me to become the expert that filled that need.

In two weeks, I was "the expert" (cue the College Humor viral YouTube clip) in serialization and armed with background on the Culture of Inclusion program. Calendar invites were sent, tickets were purchased, and I found myself on that plane to Hong Kong, where, following that initial headliner, an uneasy lack of follow-up announcements from the captain had occurred as the hours melted, lost form, and began to slide by.

Above Northern Canada, we were finally graced with the opportunity to hear our captain's update and the solution resulting from his communications with United Airlines management; never before have I heard a pilot so candid. Side note: planes do not travel straight to their destinations; rather, they often follow arcs for a number of reasons. Our plane was gracefully gliding around our little blue marble directly over the Northern Arctic Circle, eventually dipping back past the Koreas toward our final destination, and the farther we got, the more candid our pilot became in his frustration. Ultimately, the pilots announced their decision, against United's will, to conduct an emergency landing in Beijing on the merit of their own calculations, which determined the plane did not have enough fuel to make it to Hong Kong. Electrical engineering dork fun fact #1: producing more electrical power from a turbine requires an exponential amount of kinetic energy, or in this case, more jet fuel because a main turbine was down. Our pilots did not think we had enough of those dead dinos and compressed ancient veggies to make it to Hong Kong. There would be an emergency landing in Beijing. Airline management did not want it, but perhaps more importantly, the Chinese government did not want it.

It was during the seven hours on the tarmac, surrounded by our Chinese "friends" with machine guns and with nowhere to go but that blissful middle seat, that I did finally become acquainted with my fellow row-mates. From the pilots' increasingly frustrated candor, it was obvious that airline management was in the wrong, and my left-side cohort with experience in broadcasting made a prediction: the airline almost certainly had a team monitoring every single passenger on the plane – both she and the ex-salesmen to my right tweeted at the same time. Within seconds (having been flagged as a reporter for CNN on the manifest), the airline had responded to her complaint, while my friend to the right had to wait nearly ten minutes for his apologetic condolences. All customers are not created equal.

After learning I should never be a salesman in Japan if I wanted to keep my liver (so, so much alcohol), and many other "we are sitting stranded on a plane uncomfortably close together" stories, we were off. This time, it was not mechanical issues that plagued us, but FAA limits on the amount of time flight crews are allowed to work without rest. Back to his beloved microphone, our pilot said we had just minutes to take off before that limit was reached. Never had I taxied so fast in a plane, feeling it rock with each turn on the taxiway. On the runway. Ready to go. We hit the limit. With muted reluctance, clearly emanating his lost motivation, our pilot's final announcement was, "Your guess is as good as mine as to what happens next."

We could not deplane the plane. We could not get fresh food or water. We could only wait. Finally, a Beijing to Newark flight was cancelled, and their crew replaced ours. I took a two-hour nap in Hong Kong, connected to Singapore, and made it – two hours before the presentation. At headquarters, I was cordially (and simultaneously tragically) greeted with gifts of as much Pizza Hut as I could eat. My vision had the room modestly tilting back and forth, fueled by my exhaustion from nearly 42 hours of nonstop travel. Somehow, I delivered a well-received presentation. My experience there was a daze in which I took a tour of a 2 billion dollar manufacturing facility in a skyscraper, learned that North American diversity practices need to be completely retooled before launching in Asia, and visited a pharmaceutical manufacturing plant. I also spent a couple of hours enjoying the absolutely spectacular island nation of Singapore. Less than 72 hours later, I boarded another flight and landed in another island nation, Sri Lanka, for the IEEE conference.

As I will describe later, I have an absolute passion for learning from the power of international perspective, and this was my first time traveling outside of North America or Europe. I grew up just outside of Philadelphia, Pennsylvania USA in a little suburb called Haddonfield. To give you an idea of the relatively conservative stance of my parents, I had to write an essay and hold a mock judicial panel the first time I went on an international trip to stay with a host family in Germany. I had a general ignorance of other cultures, and I desired so greatly to learn more from them. It was when I walked through those hotel doors in Sri Lanka, walked down the hallway, and met another IEEE student member named Mehvish from Pakistan, that I had a truly pivotal opportunity in my life's journey to learn and evolve. This first-ever conversation with someone in a full niqab felt special – something I had never experienced before – something I was privileged to have. Frankly, it was absurd. There was no reason I should have felt that way, and I wanted to study and learn why I did, and more importantly, provide resources for everyone as sheltered as I was, to help them reach that same revelation of absurdity.

Despite this adrenaline shot in the heart of my desire to learn, I was hit with a wall of exhaustion. My official policy is to completely disregard the existence of "sleep cycles" while frolicking across so many time zones, but even riding that caffeine-melatonin sine wave, sometimes you just can't get past the jet lag. I traveled over to the elevator, met my awesome roommate Solomon, and fell asleep. I had made it to the IEEE conference, where representatives from over 15 countries had converged to talk geek, celebrate, and share experiences. In a country that less than a decade before had ended a 30-year civil war, this incredible gathering of minds and passion was convened. Over the next two days I would speak, meet lifelong friends, and sing folk songs from different countries around the world on the hotel roof with the Indian Ocean quietly pounding the beach in the background. I sang the song, "Amazing Grace".

In time for the opening ceremony, ready for action having conquered my jet lag, I stepped into an elevator – with this man: Sarang Shaikh from Pakistan.

◆◆◆

Serendipity. An English word introduced to my lexicon around 2014 when I, Sarang, was preparing for my Test of English as a Foreign Language (TOEFL) and was either required or wished to increase my vocabulary. Although the word was pretty new, it already started to make sense when I reflected on my past, and a few planned moments and happenings in particular. I can't be very certain of its root, but a teacher of mine once told me that this word was included in the dictionary by a literary scholar in the mid-17th century when he started to observe ambiguous and totally indeterminate plans and events in the life of three princes of a Persian king. The book, titled *The Three Princes of Serendip*, was published as early as the 15th century and talked about how the princes were lucky enough to land in the right places at the right times and made discoveries by accident. Every time, they met the right people that would drive their future and influence their success. After doing a little research, I also found that the word Serendip was the Old Persian name for Sri Lanka as well, even before it had been called Ceylon.

Serendipitous were the days for me when, before Sri Lanka, I met two gentlemen in Europe who were from Sri Lanka. I never had planned to and honestly didn't initially wish to meet them. Reasons for this unexpected friendship were twofold. First, I came from Pakistan, which has a friendly relationship with Sri Lanka, and so approaching like-minded people would not pose any undue difficulty. Second, I decided that since it was my first time to Europe, I would try to get a broader view of how life evolves there. My preliminary objectives were to make friends and meet European people, making my network list more transcontinental. While not European, the very first friends I made in Europe were guys named Kavinga Upul, a former PhD student, and Subodha Charles, a student about to graduate from his Bachelor's program. Little did I know that these friendships would last long, to the point where I would look back and see how that Europe trip would serendipitously result in a trip to Sri Lanka the following year; a trip where I was just not another participant, but something more.

It was in 2010 when I first joined IEEE as a student member because some of my professors and seniors recommended it to get accustomed with technical research, as IEEE has a huge repository of articles and papers published within its digital library. My initial thoughts were to try it out until I graduate, but I didn't know that this was indeed a move in the serendipitous journey that would later become an integral part of my life. Things started to make sense somehow. I got into more public-facing leadership positions at my IEEE student branch and was fortunate to receive generous funding from my school to represent the branch at different conferences around the country. It was when I graduated that I got the chance to travel to India for a student congress, which gathered people with the same passions and interests, igniting and nurturing my drive throughout my student years. The conference opened up many avenues for me. Not only did it provide me with bursts of knowledge but also developed my mental models to see the world from a wider and a more selfless perspective.

Recalling the congress, my experience from India, and how it influenced my life, I embraced the chance to experience similar moments of fanatic energy at the 2015 congress – the IEEE conference that was scheduled to happen in Sri Lanka. As a Pakistani, I have a natural propensity to like and talk about cricket. The "game of gentlemen", as it is called in Pakistan, cricket has found an almost religious eminence in south Asian countries. People don't play it, they live it. Before they reach an age where they can grasp what's best and what's not for them, kids are relatively fluent in each minutia of the rules of the game, as if to have inherited it in their blood. The success stories that we cherish are of cricket, the idols that a common young guy can have are from cricket, and cricket is truly the most admired and appreciated career pathway for anyone to pursue.

Despite partaking in the cricket craze, I was never, even to this day, any good at it. In fact, I was one of the extra guys as a kid. Whenever my neighborhood or school team went to play, they always took me for their team because they needed someone who could stay at the back to do things like: making sure everyone gets the water bottle, ensure all pads and gloves are in good condition, and assist with whatever else is required by the team or coach/senior. Although I now remember a few chances where I was asked to go and bat or bowl, it never occurred as part of the team plan. I was always part of their B-plans, so everybody knew that if I was playing, either the team wanted time to make strategic moves, or the main players were tired and wanted to rest. Sometimes they, out of pity, even asked me to go because I was a good assistant and never complained about my luck. I understood that my place was somewhere behind the pavilion, so I would be happy with at least contributing. While it sucked being that extra guy, I suppose I was best in business.

What started as an unfortunate accident soon turned itself into an opportunity. My whole childhood was spent running between grounds carrying water bottles or killing time by missing delivered match balls when the key players requested a time out. As time progressed, I became an expert at managerial work; I had kids who were junior to me now doing things that I spent my whole childhood executing. I was sort of becoming a manager who could plan matches, talk to other team managers, and even umpire matches. In my high school, I was charged with the responsibility of manager for the cricket team. Even when I was in undergraduate school, I was part of an organizing committee that hosted an annual cricket tournament for all the batches to play for a tournament cup. So I developed a reputation where cricket players needed me because they knew: this is the guy who can help us organize a tournament, umpire matches, or even be our spokesperson at tournaments in other cities.

IEEE has members from most all countries in Asia and the Pacific continents, the place where cricket is followed to an almost religious instinct. I thought: what if we have a cricket tournament during the upcoming IEEE congress, even a match between young professionals of IEEE? Certainly, not only would it be a great social activity, but it would also give everyone a chance to make more acquaintances and stronger bonds of friendship. Inopportune borders and political wills can divide us, but a game of cricket can connect. Of course, with this I also wanted to increase my cricket-managing portfolio. With this transnational match addition, I would proudly boast that not only am I good in my country, but I can host an international show, too.

Serendipity took a new turn when, out of all the countries bidding, Sri Lanka was selected to host the IEEE congress, and (you know where I am going with this) the duo Kavinga and Subodha, my Euro-trip companions, were made Chair and Secretary for the congress. I am not sure how things work outside of South Asia, but in the Desi region, if your friend sits in a position, chances are they will likely give you a favor. And perhaps it won't even be called a favor. Why? Because I am asking my friend and this is what friends do – ask! So I asked the duo initially if they thought the cricket match was a good idea. They did, and they promised they would help me organize it, but I would need to submit a proposal, plan, and guarantee that this whole headache would be mine and mine only.

I couldn't believe my wish was coming true. Ironically, the duo organized everything. They rented a local cricket ground in Colombo, and they arranged for bats, bowls, and wickets – everything that was needed. They also assisted me with some students who volunteered to take their cars and shuttle each player from the hotel to the ground and take them back afterwards. I will surely talk more about this cricket match expedition, but first we need to time-travel back to Karachi, Pakistan so we can go through the part of how my journey to Sri Lanka for the IEEE congress was accomplished in the first place.

Unlike 2013 in India, where I participated as a newbie in IEEE, the 2015 congress in Sri Lanka was different. In two years, I had developed a new interest in the Humanitarian Technology domain, and I was working alongside the team at IEEE SIGHT (Special Interest Group in Humanitarian Technology) in Karachi, initiating different projects, managing local community development programs, and reaching out to stakeholders of external societies. The IEEE congress decided to fund some of the young leaders across the Asia-Pacific to represent their SIGHT activities and involve them in a discussion with seasoned social entrepreneurs and leaders. I was selected. This is how I financed my trip. Not only had I embarked on my serendipity-fueled journey to the country that was previously called Serendip, but I was also accompanied by students and young professionals all sharing each other's ambitions.

On the way to Sri Lanka for the congress, we took one direct Sri Lankan Air flight to the capital, Colombo. Again in surprise fashion, on our way to what would be my first international cricket match, we ran into none other than Sri Lankan Cricket Legend Sanath Jayasuriya at the Karachi Airport before boarding. In his era, he had attained the world record for the fastest century, pulling off 100 in just 48 balls within a day match against Pakistan. As a kid, I hated watching this guy score a world record against the Pakistani side, but things turned upside down when a Pakistani emerging player named Shahid Afridi scored the then fastest century in just 37 balls against the Sri Lankan side. Anyway, let bygones be bygones; all Pakistanis admire Sanath Jayasuriya's services to our nation. More than being an excellent sportsman, his role in combating the terror scene and bringing new boys to our land to play friendly matches left an impact. We tried to take a picture with him, but before we could grasp the opportunity, he was swamped with a group of people asking for autographs and photographs. While we also wanted any sort of evidence that he could give to record the moment, we weren't quite so lucky.

Reaching Sri Lanka at midnight was fun in itself. We took a taxi for an almost hour-long journey to Colombo's finest hotel, where we decided to settle for three days to talk, discuss, and share knowledge while utilizing IEEE's resources and multi-layer networks. Soon we were done with registration, and I met my roommate, an Indian guy named Nivas Ravichandran, who would later become one of my good friends. As soon as I told him, "You're here in this room with me," he breathed a sigh of relief and thanked me for saving his time and efforts in finding where the heck he would crash for the night.

The sun rose. Pumped up with excitement, I couldn't stay in my room at all. I threw my luggage open, changed my clothes, and surged downstairs like a king who was going to give some of the selected ones an experience of a lifetime by organizing a cricket match. But the jet lag took hold of me, as I hadn't slept the whole night, too excited by the upcoming cricket match.

The cricket match was everything I could have dreamed of. Two teams with both female and male players, equally talented, were formed. The match lasted a short but amazing 6 overs that drew interest until the second team's one player, a Sri Lankan himself named Dinuka, started raining sixes and made a score that won the whole match. And then it was time for this (now international) cricket manager to jump into the conference – the IEEE congress for which I had come to Sri Lanka. In time for the opening ceremony, ready for action, I stepped into an elevator – with this man: Jeff Eker.

◆◆◆

Anyone will tell you that a successful elevator pitch is one that forges an interest in pursuing the next conversation. Our journey – Sarang's and mine – is one forged from those simple introductions in an elevator. We have both, before and since, traveled the world.

Action Items Related to Chapter One

1. Go to an interesting place or event. Introduce yourself to and learn about the life of three complete strangers – send them something as a follow-up (a TEDx video, a networking connection, etc.) in relation to your conversation that adds value to a pursuit or passion of theirs you learned about.

2. Watch the same video or a movie that was produced in a country other than your own in two different languages you do not speak without subtitles; guess the meaning or context of conversations based on expressions and gestures. Afterwards, turn on subtitles to compare how accurately you predicted what they were saying.

Part One

Before the Elevator

Jeffrey Eker Jr. & Sarang Shaikh

2: THE FISHBOWL

Lesson: There is a difference between interacting with and learning from the world around you. Take nothing for granted.

It was a happy time. I absentmindedly stared across the field of brownish-green grass that hung in a gray, hazy space in the sandy soil nearby Lewis, Delaware, USA. Across that field, dotted with PVC pipes where the new homes were to be built, was ours — for the week, at least. Every year since I could remember, we would drive a couple hours south to meet family at the beach, the great escape. That year we were lucky to get a big house for a discount as it was a brand new construction and they had to build a reputation for the property, we were told. I whirled my personal cognition back, zooming my near surroundings back into focus and looked across the pool.

We needed that big house. Surrounding me was the family I love: my mom, dad, sister, aunt, uncle, other aunt, cousin, her husband, their less-than-year-old son, and my grandmom. There was nothing but smiles; we even convinced my grandmom to hop in the swimming pool. We were all, for the most part, an overweight bunch just living our own little version of the American dream. After cooking burgers, we encapsulated the moment in the pool by spelling out "Lewis" with neon-colored foam floating pool noodles. An avid book reader, my mom demanded — on account of the sometimes lazy, sometimes pool-fight euphoria of the moment that had lasted the past couple hours — that we write a book, "Tons of Fun": an honest quip at our family's obesity.

That week was tons of fun. As with every year, I begged to race go-karts, and this year my cousin's husband Jon was the first to agree, and we hit the track. There were trips to Candy Kitchen, where soft-water toffee and fudge were purchased, and to the Texas Roadhouse restaurant where the peanut shells that littered the ground crunched as we headed to our bountiful steak dinners. Every member of my family, myself included, will certainly smile reading this as they recall the memory.

There was a reason for that discount on the rental, and those PVC pipes, where houses should have been developed, however. It was 2010, and while I was ignorant to it at the time, the United States was in the midst of the great recession. I was incredibly lucky to have a truly perfect nuclear family, with my mom and dad sacrificing a great deal of their time and financial means to ensure that my sister and I got an amazing education and could continue to climb the social mobility ladder as they had done over their lifetimes. It was around the time when I was applying for colleges that my dad sat me down and with an awkward passion asked me to continue the hard work that he had strived for. Starting in a relatively poor family, he had made it to the upper middle class, and I would have to fight to continue that upward trend. It wouldn't be easy, but I had to do it; I said I would, and I meant it. As perfect as our family was, those serious conversations were the one thing we never quite figured out how to open up during. As always, the couch was soft and the leaves were green outside the window when my parents told me that Jon, who I rode those go-karts with only two months before, had hung himself, leaving my cousin and their less than one-year-old son behind. Jon was a construction worker and felt that the stress of not finding work and not being able to support the family during that Great Recession was too much. Just months later, we learned their son Cole would be wheelchair-bound by age 12, diagnosed with Duchenne Muscular Dystrophy, for which there is no cure and would limit his life expectancy to early adulthood.

Sometimes the only way to move forward is to say that life goes on. For many people, I think that this is the best way to digest challenges and continue on. For me, it was a drive that I knew I could not take life for granted. I felt incredibly motivated to better myself and pursue success, to take advantage of how lucky I was to be surrounded by incredible people.

Those people, and myself at the time, were dorks. Amazing dorks. Have you ever heard of a program called "Odyssey of the Mind"? Look it up. I was in it for six years and was proud to go to the World Finals Tournament all six years. I have a bath towel full of pins from around the world that I traded from those competitions, and I owe so much of my personality and creativity to my friends and mentors who followed me throughout that journey.

Have you heard of a marching band? For those outside of the US who may not know much about it, look that one up, too. For four years I played the saxophone in the marching band and again was surrounded by some of the best band geeks one could ask for, capping the experience off by being the Drum Major (the leader that conducts the band) during my fifth year.

While after school I was a HOOTM (Haddonfield Odyssey of the Mind) dork and by evening and weekends in the fall I was a band geek, most of the time I was a super cool Boy Scout. I had been doing that all the way since kindergarten, and in 2011, I was the Senior Patrol Leader of Troop 3065 and on the fast track to becoming an Eagle Scout. Just about once a month for the past 11 years, I had found myself going on a camping trip with the Boy Scouts, and over the years had found myself in a plethora of incredible situations. Every year we would go to summer camp and over several trips found myself backpacking in the Adirondack and Catskill Mountains, and over 100 miles of the

Appalachian Trail. During a two-week trip to Philmont, New Mexico, I even rolled down a mountain, had a bear steal my boot, and saw people almost go into hypothermia. I had learned a lot and was excited to be one of only four percent who actually made it all the way to the Eagle Scout rank.

I got to wear costumes for Odyssey of the Mind performances and a colonial uniform for marching band competitions. That was great, don't get me wrong, but neither of those had badges. My Boy Scout uniform had lots of badges, and I looked pretty badass with them on. I did not actually have to wear all the parts of the Boy Scout uniform to almost any occasion really, but when I did, it was called my "Class A" uniform. All pieces included my merit badge sash (tucked into the belt to make way for my Order of the Arrow sash, embodying the secret honor society of Boy Scouts), Order of the Arrow sash crossing diagonally over my chest, meticulously tightly-wound neckerchief, leather-stamped Philmont belt with a giant bull belt buckle from Nashville, olive green Boy Scout shorts with fleur-de-lis metal snaps, green socks with the red band on the top, and the hiking boots that had literally been branded with the Philmont logo in New Mexico.

On a frightful Monday morning back in 2011, some German exchange students were coming into town. To properly understand the occasion, you have to first properly understand the town. I grew up in the epitome of a "mom and pop" town: two square miles, no school buses because you can walk everywhere, a dinosaur statue, and a rich colonial history. When the foreigners came, it was your classic hometown politics ensuring that all the parents were involved. The mayor even showed up, and you are darned right, I was going to be a part of it and make an impact! My best friend Jared and I had a well-devised plan: we were going to impress those Germans with our Class A uniforms. After all, the welcome ceremony started in the high school library right after the Boy Scout meeting, and there was simply no way that we would have time to change and make it to the ceremony anywhere close to on time.

We rolled in like the true unequivocally dorky bad asses we were, and, in the heat of the moment, with self-confidence at some astronomical level unseen before, I turned to Jared and said, "I'm going to introduce myself to the prettiest girl in the room." I did; her name was Angie. More on that later.

The German teacher facilitating this trip was both a notorious and illustriously loved man by the name of Herr Christopher Gwin. In middle school we were given the option to take one of three languages, and in sixth grade, one third of the year was dedicated to each of those languages so that you could decide which one you would choose to stick with through the course of seventh and eighth grade. Spanish was too mainstream, French was too hard to pronounce, and the German teacher offered me candy... so the rest is history. I glided through seventh and eighth grade like a breeze, singing happily "Ich bin ein Auslander und sprech man nicht gut Deutsch *ding* *ding*," eating pretzels, watching laughable old videos, and generally learning somewhere between retaining a few words to pretty much retaining nothing after the quiz. In high school, I was in for a rude awakening.

On the first day of German class in high school, Herr Gwin kindly proceeded to begin teaching – completely in German. The whole time. He gave us some Hausaufgaben (homework) and sent us on our way. For the next four years, this man literally only spoke English when he was vehemently enraged at the class or offering his time as the instructor of the color guard for the marching band. I have never met a more creative, dedicated, forward-thinking, and impactful teacher in my life. Since that time, I have known more friends and classmates who have gone on to travel to Germany, live in Germany, pursue degrees in Germany, and even marry Germans than I can count. In no other instance have I met anyone who can gladly say they, along with everyone who went through the program, became fluent in a language during high school.

Despite the incessant long homework assignments forcing us to attempt reading through current events around the world or preparing for debates speaking only German on capital punishment, we slogged through. Most importantly, however, we had become super interested in German girls. Now, a lesson on the European emoji game. Sending so much as a winky face in the United States pretty much intimates that you're looking to get it on. In Europe? It could mean anything from absolutely nothing to I just made a joke. We did not know this, and, little to our knowledge at the time, it would lead to some pretty crushing romantic defeats in my group of friends down the line. Regardless, we knew we had to make it to Germany.

Most high schools in the United States have what is known as a senior trip. In an opulent, first world fashion, my entire senior class hopped on a plane and flew to Disney World, or at least that was the plan. My friends Jared, Andrew, and I had a different plan: fly to Germany, spend twice as long traveling than the Disney World excursion, and save $200 in the process. Foolproof, right? Wrong.

My parents had other thoughts. In many ways I do not blame them for the way they were thinking, or really most American parents who have not had the opportunity to embrace other cultures. In the end, you could honestly spend your whole life visiting different places in the US and die with plenty more left to see. For them, sending their son abroad to stay with a family they had never met, in a foreign country that my grandmom still thought was dangerous, when I was below the American-contrived legal drinking age of 21, was a terrible idea. After weeks of back and forth, it finally came down to a convening of a multi-family pitch session.

As the sun hit the horizon and the upper middle class scuttled about in the red-brick laden downtown paradise of Haddonfield, New Jersey, the council of parents convened under the gazebo next to the favorite homey, yet overpriced, town ice cream shop in a pedestrian walkway where dress, cake, and toy shops lined either side. The American flag quietly tapped and hugged the flag pole as Andrew, Jared, and I tilted our heads to look up at our parents arranged on benches before us – desperate to make our final case. In the end they gave in. At the time it was really all about the girls for us and the excitement of a trip overseas, but when January rolled around, it became much more for me. In March of 2012, I would board that plane with Jared and Andrew, but in the lead-up to those wheels leaving the runway, three months before, I would hear a word that would come to define my life.

Following that continued drive to push and challenge myself to improve where I saw personal weakness, I had enrolled in the Advanced Preparation English Composition course. Structured by a birth child of the American ingenuity behind profiting from education, AP courses are college-level courses that allow students to highly curve their high school grade point averages for college applications and challenge themselves more than their peers. In this case, it truly was very challenging because ever since first grade and being placed in a struggling small group of kids trying to learn English, my skills in the area had never been sharp, and suddenly, I was tasked by our teacher, Ms. Vermaat, to write an entire essay on the definition of one word. What?!

How do you write an entire essay on the definition of one word? More importantly, which word do you choose? I went to all my friends, family, and teachers, asking which word they thought would be best to write an essay on. I got cool words, words with dual meanings, and words that were fun to say as I frantically went about trying to find the absolute best word to develop a standout essay. It wasn't until I went back and asked Angie from our German Exchange Program, the cutie from the library who months before pretended not to be freaked out by some weirdo in a paramilitary uniform (me in my Boy Scout uniform), that I got the answer I was looking for. Several months after initially meeting in the high school library during the opening ceremony for the exchange, we had grown close – helping each other learn each other's language. Communicating daily on Skype, I was accustomed to her brisk, snappy responses and became a bit concerned when it took her a long time to respond to my question about the perfect word.

Finally, she responded "Miracle", citing in somewhat broken English, "In the end, it is all the small things in life that we take for granted all around us that are most important and create little miracles every day." I paused, a bit taken aback. Incredible. All I had to do was take one step out of the fishbowl of my hectic society to someone peering into it, trying to learn about my society and culture, to understand what was valuable all around me.

It is true that such insight would help shape my perspective in understanding just how privileged I was to be in that swimming pool back in Lewis, having tons of fun. To have parents who sacrificed so much financially to move to a town where I could have an incredible education, where I could lead the Boy Scout troop and the marching band, as well as travel to six Odyssey of the Mind world finals tournaments. To understand just how lucky I was to be born on a sandbar built from the erosion of the Appalachian Mountains called New Jersey in a country with so much wealth and opportunity. These were my miracles. From that point on, it became my career ambition to spread the power of international perspective, and it is that career ambition that would define my drive for years to come.

Action Items Related to Chapter Two

1. Watch the movie "The Big Short" to understand what US culture was like around the time of the financial recession when I was in that pool on our family beach vacation.

2. Read, watch, or listen to the same story published by three different news sources on the internet and try to identify what differs in how the information is conveyed.

3: PILGRIMAGE AND SAUDI EVENINGS

Lesson: Deferring your happiness to worldly materials and future times is a bad idea; living in the present requires a check-back on life. A journey to the right destination can bring this revelation.

International exposure and cultural mind shifts are concepts for which I had never had an understanding until I traveled for the very first time on a journey, along with my family, that not only changed my hypothesis on the world but also provided an opportunity to look over the world from more than 10,000 feet above, immersed in layers of clouds. Beheld with an eagle eye view, I made my first-ever trip on an international flight to Saudi Arabia in 2011. My childhood was studded with surreal memories brought about by my father, who made me travel on short, domestic airplane flights back when having a plane ticket would require one to change into a full three-piece suit and be considered lucky in Pakistan. Nonetheless, growing up I couldn't help but daydream of how it would be to fly a long distance at a very high altitude – it surely was a luxury, a mode of transport for the rich was what I had heard all my life. As we rode in to catch our flight from the mighty-sized Karachi International Airport, my heart pumped to its maximum beat and I couldn't hold my excitement. Fortunately, living near Karachi Airport, almost all my early youthful evenings were spent counting the number of flights flown over my house. Unfortunately, most of my parents' middle-aged evenings were spent welcoming relatives and friends, either dropping them off or picking them up from the airport, where I happily followed my father with whatever course of action he was undertaking. Walking across the terminals and airport building always impressed me. The sheer size of the airport impressed me too, and running back and forth on escalators was always fun as they were not common back then, as they were only found at the airport in Pakistan.

Mark Twain wrote that "Travel is the death of prejudice." For sure, this does not stand true for all travel, but it only takes a few travel experiences to reinforce your belief, building into a more substantial mindset that doesn't value prejudice. One particular type of travel is a pilgrimage journey; it is this spiritual practice of pilgrimage that cuts across all cultures and is practiced in almost all religions. This holy journey carries multiple meanings, as for some it is the search for God, some others take it to find the meaning of existence and life, while some also go through it to rejuvenate into new practices, finding their lost souls in their humdrum lives. I don't know which of the above intentions I had as I flew with my family to Saudi Arabia to perform Umrah (a Muslim pilgrimage, a holy journey to Makkah and Madina), but certainly whichever it was, it transformed me into a changed person. Not only did I identify more exposure opportunities and ways to open more mental avenues, but it also it gave me the feeling of living globalized for the very first time in my life.

I remember, as we walked into the airport, I had a sense of achievement. Although it sounds juvenile and meaningless for someone like me who grew up imagining traveling in airplanes and experiencing life among the fluffy, white clouds, this first time felt like a lifetime achievement. Along with my family, I cleared the security checks and tried to look cool by mimicking and following what fellow passengers were doing. As we walked into our boarding room, I walked around and peeked into glorious shops to sense an upscale shopping touch – even the restrooms felt like the ones in 5-star hotels. Looking at the magnificence of the airport and the diversity of people in it, I pondered thoughts that were deep enough to hibernate in.

Belonging to a mid-level income family, I hadn't experienced a luxurious life as a child and often had to struggle for petty things. Completing chores big and small for my house was my way of contributing back to the family. There were, in fact, times as a kid when I had to do street-side businesses such as: selling stickers for a slight margin of profit in the neighborhood, run a potato chips counter down the street, and even trade computer video game CDs with kids in surrounding localities. All of these little opportunities provided big benefits, which for sure included profit that was extra pocket money and recognition among kids, bridging their access to markets. Fortunately, the economic conditions of Pakistan have significantly improved over the years, and thus the comparative meaning of mid-level income has also transformed. Today, even kids from mid-level families are carried in personal cars to and from school. They don't have to undertake many struggles to augment their little treasure, and the concept of running businesses has changed, now being termed as a "start-up". Also today, the Intergovernmental Organizations and global institutions have put much work and effort into countries like Pakistan, making travel easier and enabling cultural diversity to take flight. The emergence of organizations such as **AIESEC** (Association Internationale des Étudiants en Sciences Économiques et Commerciales) and **Rotary Fellowships**, which encourage students to travel and spend time in other parts of the world by volunteering their skills, have exposed Pakistan's citizens to things that are opposite of what they have seen or have studied, further emboldening an appreciation for diversity.

Being a millennial myself, I spent my childhood in the late 1990s and early 2000s. Back then, traveling was not only expensive but also difficult. Besides, the mere thought of traveling was restricted to formal business work, and no teenage or youth considered traveling in planes for fun. Also, the internet was not widespread, and technology was not as ubiquitous as it is today, so any millennial kid's chances were very slim to get a view of how life worked outside of their country – to understand what globalization really looked and felt like. The only means which uncovered the aspects of global life were TV and movies. I was a fan of Hollywood movies, and watching them made me feel mixed thoughts, both happy and sad. Happy because I enjoyed watching the new things in them and sad because I was not able to experience them. I remember once I watched the movie *Home Alone*, and the kid acting in it was almost the same age as me. The cryptic things he did and how he spent his childhood staying in luxurious hotels and living wealthy always made me contemplate thoughts like: how does an average kid spend their time in a foreign land, how do the rich kids live life, and what does it feel like to be rich?

The eccentric sensation those movies provided me were enough to daydream through life without any mental boundaries. I saw movies where the good guy would meet his dream girl sitting beside him on a plane or train, and their lives would unfold into new directions from then on. I watched movies where guys had so many homes and friends that wherever he went he had a place to stay and had friends to mingle with and a multitude of opportunities that cheered, encouraged, and expanded his involvement with the global community. Growing up watching all that stuff and not being able to travel internationally, I developed some mental models on how globalization worked and had already dreamt so many times of myself enacting the life of a character that sees only physical boundaries, not mental. I wanted to experience life outside of my country, a dream realized in 2011 on this family trip.

Awakened from the slumber of a life built on rewinding thoughts, I realized our flight to Saudi Arabia had been called for boarding. We sprinted towards our seats. I intentionally did not want to sit with my family to have the opportunity of luck to find my dream girl, the heroine of my life that would meet me here and change my life afterwards. Not only was I excited to see who would join me for a window seat, but my family was equally interested as they knew my intentions of sitting separately. In my empty room and in front of the mirror, I had acted out multiple times the "romantic talk" that I would speak with my dream girl, and while I was already rehearsing that for the flight, a hand shoved my shoulder, and it was a middle-aged guy (I would probably say uncle) with a fat bulging tummy and goatee-style beard asking me to move aside as this seat belonged to him. My family made sure to embarrass me by giggling all the way and pointing directions like "behold, your beauty or the beast has arrived." I was flabbergasted as my only chance was in vain, and I had to bear this guy for rest of my trip.

Never having flown on a jet plane before (only propeller planes), I feared the altitude would get the better of me and my acrophobic nature would jump into overdrive. I waited anxiously and looked out of the window as the plane taxied away, nearing the runway. Before I knew it, the engines had taken over and the impact of takeoff pushed me back into the seat while the plane pierced between clouds towards its destination.

Surely it is near impossible to fathom the immensity of how big the world is in terms of area and cultural diversity without travel. Traveling has its own means of experiencing things first-hand, different from imagining how it would be or actually is in movies or in pictures. While munching on my lunch and feeling self-pity for my bad luck of sitting at my seat beside an uncle, we landed at Dubai Airport in UAE in a short time, where we had to switch planes for Jeddah toward Saudi Arabia. For anyone who has spent their life believing that airports are small buildings connected to largely spaced runways and hangers, the vastness of Dubai International Airport will give you chills. I was amazed, yet distressed, looking at the size of this airport. It had many terminals, each of which had many gates, and each gate had many counters. It took us time to comprehend exactly our spot and find our connecting flight. After settling in, our next flight from Dubai to Jeddah started with prayer. "Ladies and gentlemen," the flight attendant said over the intercom, "the script that you will all hear in a minute is a supplication that the Prophet Mohammed (peace be upon him) used to pray before traveling."

Expecting the same luck with the uncle on the previous flight, I didn't bother much making acquaintance with yet another middle-aged man until the plane was about to land. We exchanged a few words, however, which ended with him giving me some tips on how to not fade out and still enjoy the weather in the severely heat-laden, scorching days of Saudi Arabia. The usual days reach around 40-45 degrees Celsius on average. While there I observed that while tourists reclined under the inexorable afternoon sun, local Saudis would often retire indoors or to a sheltered spot for a siesta – kind of a power nap that refills the body and mind with new energy. Although the heat did get ahold of me, I decided not to become too comfortable by spending an unproductive afternoon relaxing. Instead, I busied myself with pilgrimage rituals, prayers, and readings of the Holy Book, as well as other relevant practices.

Religious pilgrimages grow out of the yearning to associate one's own self with a holy place in the tradition. The place itself is so invigorating, it never feels tiring or exhausting, even spending whole days performing rituals and spending a greater part of the evening and night to pray. The number of people you come across at such religious places or shrines is enormous. Everyone has their own version of the story to tell; they come with different human particulars but are all bonded with the same vigor and passion to thank God for His blessings.

Time accelerated quickly, as if I had just arrived today. I met a few people and made contacts with whom I would meet in the evenings and spend time chatting. Those small talks that I had with random strangers gave me an entirely new sense of belonging. We spent two weeks in the cities of Makkah where the Prophet was born. Indeed, the religion was born here, in this city, in the western part of Saudi Arabia better known as Madina. Dressed up in mandatory clothing called Ehram (for men) was something of a challenge for me. Every man has to wear Ehram – white garment clothes wrapped around your body. It's not just wearing it that makes you honorable, rather it also acts as a conduit to get your body and mind to transform into a dedicated sacred state aimed with the intention of performing the pilgrimage. It is forbidden to wear any sewn garment, and thus Ehram also symbolizes the unity of humankind and faith, imparting a lesson that we all might have forgotten and look to convert by several means, but rather it is more of a revert that we need to get back to what's common in all of us humans: the body and soul. We can always talk about differences, but what's common with us is our feelings. We are different yet the same, and this spree of globalization that has emerged in the past few decades has made it possible to justify that we are all indeed the same, just guided by different principles and rules.

Apart from the sweat-drenched, heat-filled days and the pilgrimage visitor's facade, what's interesting is the local food and Arabic cuisine. Saudi Arabia offers a much-varied landscape of food options, more than we could have imagined. I did hear about a few foods in Pakistan like shawarma and hummus, but I got the real mouthwatering taste of it while staying there. The other foods that I had the pleasure of eating were za'atar (a flavored mix of different things on bread mostly), taamia (a sandwich wrap of veggies), and a variety of things sold by supermarkets with unique names such as the Danube and Hyper Panda, and the list goes on. Al-Baik was nearly the Saudi-equivalent of KFC in the US. Nevertheless, when I came back, I realized and was informed by friends that what I think I tasted was not even Saudi-originated food. I am still waiting to go again and try them all out. However, during the travel to Saudi Arabia, I straightaway understood why our subcontinent back in 18th century or so had built a reputation of spice production. It was ironic to know that the British colonized the region for merely acquiring the hold of spices and for similar reasons. Eating spicy food through my childhood in Pakistan, I never understood the importance of it, and while studying the reasons of such, it was quite difficult to grasp the fact that the British came for that reason and built the whole empire on it. Surely the historians must be joking, right? It can't just be for spices, can it?

This concept finally made sense when I was thrown off by the less-spicy food in Saudi Arabia, and in fact, the spiciest that they offered was way less than my threshold. My taste buds have developed a flavor of spice, and whenever I eat something less than that, I eat too quickly. Besides, the number one rule of eating while foreign traveling is definitely to try everything, you never know when you will get the chance again. Further, you get a comparative sense of what your food is worth back home. Later on in my life, I tried different foods that were tastier than Pakistani dishes. Though they weren't much spicier, the flavor itself was a treat, and gradually I developed my taste buds with time. I have had great experiences with different foods that I have tasted around the world.

What's interesting is to study how food and eating cultures develop the upsurge of globalization. Just merely by looking at western outlets here in Pakistan such as McDonald's, KFC, and Pizza Hut being the old guard of the group, I now see newly launched ones such as

Dunkin Donuts, Subway, and Texas Steak refining their dishes as per Pakistani values. The milky tea + badaam (almond) donut would be the best deal in Pakistani Dunkin Donuts, but surely that would change when you order it anywhere else. I remember when I tried to order milk tea the first time in Dunkin Donuts in the USA, I couldn't understand who was right and who was not. The tea didn't have milk at all. Later I learned that this is how milk tea is served, and my reaction was "where's the milk in it?" But since Pakistani people have had a habit of drinking tea with a lot of milk in it for ages, we somehow want milk in every hot drink.

The pilgrimage came to an end after two weeks, and I moved along with my family to a more cosmopolitan city, Jeddah. While staying there, I found that there was a TEDx Jeddah event scheduled on the same days as our visit. Looking to grab at this good opportunity, I emailed the organizers and they happily invited me to attend the event which I later did; it was my first ever TEDx event participation. I met people there that were surely Saudi nationals, but I couldn't understand the fact: who was the real Saudi? The ones that I met in regions such as Makkah and Madina, or the ones I met in Jeddah, who happen to seem more cultivated and globally-oriented citizens? I can definitely say my observations could have been wrong and biased since that was my first ever trip abroad, and I myself was not too developed and educated. But the initial thoughts almost bewildered me upon understanding the real essence of the Saudi Arabian people and culture.

What started as an excitement ended quickly, and soon the traveling days came to an end, as I went back to Karachi with life lessons that had shaped me into a good human. This expedition was enough to stimulate my mental concepts and motivate me to travel and meet more people around the world, to finally become a "global citizen".

Action Items Related to Chapter Three

1. Get an understanding of the basic key beliefs of the two most practiced world religions other than your own. Write some common/mutual points between them and your religion. (Hint - talk to someone from the other religion on peace, marriage rituals, festivals etc.).

2. Attend a religious ceremony from a different religion.

3. Eat three different dishes that you have never had before - what did you find different from the normal food you enjoy regarding the flavor, spice-level, and taste?

4: THE AUSTRALIAN-AMERICAN IEEE STUDENT BRANCH EXCHANGE

Lesson: Attaining power while studying as an undergraduate is easy. Take it. Finding a power vacuum for something you're passionate about is as easy as creating one.

I remember exactly where I was, walking the streets of Berlin talking geek about IEEE, when a big, tall, lanky guy behind me said with a big smile, "IEEE? I just started an IEEE student branch!" Matt was studying electrical and computer engineering at James Cook University in Australia. We both found ourselves in Germany, studying abroad at the International Winter University in Kassel, Hessen, where we were acting on our passion for both engineering and the opportunity to learn from other cultures. We both realized that, while it was great we were learning so much, we were only two. How could we find a way to spread the opportunity to learn from varying cultural perspectives to others? What if we created an international partnership between our two universities? What if we executed joint competitions, projects, and seminars? What if we conveyed the value proposition enough to physically send a group of students to meet the students at the other university? We did all of the above.

The summer after my senior year of high school, it was my second internship at the Naval Surface Warfare Center, Carderock Division. While all of my other friends did things like go to the beach and generally have fun doing normal teenager summer activities, I was quite comfortable happily dorking away at my sensor network node box and data acquisition system test rig; it was all in good fun. The leader of that Science and Engineering Apprenticeship Program (SEAP) was Kimberly Drake, who has unfortunately since passed. Kimberly was fierce – she was aggressively overweight, relatively unkempt, and extremely passionate about everything she did. Exactly the type of person I was happy to avoid, staying in my blissful, relatively uneventful, stereotypically government, dorky hands-on data acquisition role. One day she asked me to come by her office.

I wound my way through the truly maze-like World War II-era building to her cube, where I was greeted by another SEAP, Gina – who, as she walked away, said "Hi!" with a big smile. Kimberly informed us that, as we were both going to Rowan University, we were to start an American Society of Naval Engineers (ASNE) club there. Having not yet started college myself, I wanted to avoid any commitments beforehand, and so I had been doing my best to ward off any obligations. To my horror, Gina (entering her second year of undergraduate) immediately signed us up. It was genius.

Why it was genius lies solely in the hands of the American higher education system. There are more than 3,000 colleges and universities in the United States, and each one of them needs to be better than everyone else for at least one reason – but preferably a multitude of reasons – to attract the best students. While a high school senior, for example, I literally filled an oven-sized bucket full of the mailer materials sent to my house, and my parents spent thousands of dollars touring me around the country to different universities trying to decide where I would go. Gina saw the value proposition and knew, perhaps as a result of her being there for a year, that the Rowan College of Engineering was thirsty for industry partnerships, and she was starting with a direct connection to one. What's more, she would be the leader of the organization and control an entire club. It was the perfect CV resume-building vehicle.

Through ASNE, I attended my first ever professional conference. We grew the club over time, and scored a reasonable budget while fostering the industry connection Gina had laid the groundwork for from the college to NAVSEA. But I had missed my shot. Gina had made all the big actions, and while the continuity of leadership we had established would continue to grow that ASNE club, the club was just a sapling organization, and the impact I could achieve at its helm was minimal. While ASNE was multi-disciplinary, attracting members across multiple engineering majors, the IEEE club was not. IEEE was my discipline's cornerstone club for extracurricular activity, and I was impressed by the number of people that participated and the amount of activities that went on.

As such, there was quite a bit of "old guard" and politicking that went on within the IEEE club. Everyone cozied up to the club's executive board throughout the year, and two candidates mustered up their support structures in public shows, fortifying their candidacy for the chair position. The elections for all clubs were coming up, and I needed to make a choice: whether to become the chair of ASNE or vie for the IEEE club's chair position, which would give me the same type of resume powerhouse that Gina had achieved with ASNE. I realized that universities wanted industry partnership, but so too did students – they wanted internships and jobs – and I knew how to help students get them based on the multiple internships I had been completing since high school. With the other two candidates in full-on campaign mode, I silently began my strategic communications. These included joining a hackathon team with the current chair and a past chair, making some backroom mentions about some things I could accomplish, and submitting my candidacy literally in the last hour before the deadline. Of the initial two candidates, one had emerged above the other, and seeing me as a last-minute non-threat, he gave a great speech erring on the side of continued greatness and fluff for the position he was sure to achieve. A classic "there will be comfort in the status quo" routine. There is no other way to describe it except to say that I dark-horsed the shit out of that room. In other words, the audience was caught completely off-guard. I gave a compelling, motivated, and serious vision of establishing the growing success of the club based on industry partnerships. It worked, and I was elected as chair of the IEEE club. As I later came to learn through lobbying the United States Congress in Washington, DC, it is very true that there is one thing that always wins elections: jobs. In parallel with campaigning for chair of the IEEE club, I was also campaigning for a different opportunity. More on that later.

I began building credibility for my campaign promises by participating on the sponsorship committee for an IEEE student activities conference in 2014, the largest of its kind in the area, hosted annually. This time, the conference was going to be held at my own university, Rowan. As I was learning, it turned out that industry has a hard time finding new graduates to fill jobs and would spend thousands of dollars going out to different universities trying to find a couple of students that would fit the bill. Good news, our conference was bringing all of the students from several dozen universities to one place, and for a small sponsorship dollar value, those companies could come recruit right from our conference. It was easy. Money was pouring in, and that's what finally got me noticed in the Dean's office – for all the wrong reasons. Remember that thirst for industry connections I was telling you about? It turns out that the university had a well-oiled fundraising machine for these industry connections, and I was raising so much money that it actually popped up on their radar as a disrupter for some of the careful politicking they were working on for the bigger, much larger potential investments. I got a slap on the wrist, but more importantly they started thinking of me as a serious proponent for the college, and now as chair of the IEEE student branch club, I had a vehicle with which to act on it.

That IEEE Student Activities Conference went very well, and I was able to launch myself into the highest student position attainable in the entire IEEE organization, providing me international visibility and responsibility. The first of many IEEE missions: accomplished.

In the years before the Student Activities Conference was held at Rowan in 2014, the conference was as much as a $35,000 expense for IEEE. By the time I would eventually graduate from Rowan, it had become a $7,000+ profit driver. That's great, but it's not worth much surprise. Raising money was something I was good at, but the drive to do so was fueled mainly by my passion for spreading the power of international perspective I had nurtured since that definition essay in high school (remember the word "miracle"?).

"It is challenging to study abroad as an engineer" might as well have been chiseled into the walls of the engineering building at Rowan. The unique curriculum made it difficult to spend a semester abroad. But, good news, you could always indulge in one of the study abroad rackets through third-party companies during the summer! This was massively expensive, and I was determined to make money, not spend it, during the summer through internships. After months of researching, finally, I found the opportunity I was looking for: the International Winter University at Universität Kassel. The problem? It was unapproved. I remember sitting in the study abroad office at Rowan looking through a binder and saying "This one looks great, but I'm an engineer – I guess I won't be able to do it." Bureaucratically, "No," they replied. The conversation insatiably grinded on: "Well, I have this great program that fits into winter break! I can add it to the approved list," I said. "No," they replied, "only the programs in the binder are approved." Having planned for the scripted bureaucratic revolving door, I pointedly asked, "How about this one? How did it get in the binder?" They were no match for me. If it was in the binder, it had to have gotten there somehow, sometime, and I was getting mine right there along beside them. It took three months, countless emails, and a couple of meetings, but I found myself enrolled and sent my first ever international wire transfer to register. To rub it in, I milked the program for everything I could get – the three-week accelerated program ended up counting for: two German courses, two honors concentration courses, and an electrical engineering elective. You have got to love it. Victory is sweet. Studying abroad is incredible. I highly recommend everyone does it at some point (or multiple) in their academic career.

It was while I was studying at the International Winter University that I met Matt on the streets of Berlin and we began talking. We both shared a raw, genuine passion for connecting people around the world. He as founder and myself as chair of our respective IEEE student branches, we kicked off an international partnership. Matt was on the outgoing end of things, having founded the IEEE student branch, so I was connected with their new chair, Ashley. Ashley and I navigated the insane 14-hour difference between us to begin meeting once a week. He was a driver in the managerial sense, and while we built our student branch's success on networking and soft skills, he was building his program on the technical side around a sumo robot competition. As it turns out, this was the perfect template for an international competition that could be tied into our partnership.

What is a sumo robot competition? Yes, everyone wanted to know; it was quite catchy. Little four-by-four inch sumo robots fought in rounds to push each other out of a one meter diameter ring. They could be bought as kits, and aside from coding your tactics for pushing the other robot out of the ring, just about the only other thing that could be changed was the gear ratio in the motors. This meant that the first-ever Rowan University Sumo Robot Competition had not only several local universities competing, but also our international partners on the other side of the world. They emailed us their gear ratio and code ahead of time; we soldered in the motors, loaded up the code, and made the locals news that night on channel six. It was a fantastic success and ran in parallel with several other projects and seminars as part of the partnership.

As far as maintaining my campaign promise, it was right in line. For decades, companies have been globalizing, and the formula for doing so is relatively generic at this point. The challenge comes in finding qualified applicants who understand what a global company is, why it is, and how it operates. How do you become the perfect applicant for a company looking to engage that talent? Perhaps, travel to another country – live with families to understand the culture, shadow students in classes to understand their academics, and visit various industry locations to get an idea of their professional culture. We now had the tools and ability to pull this off on a global scale with our new partner school in Australia, and had a set of academic and industry backers to get us started. The plan was made, and the goal was set: send ten students to Australia that summer.

In a way we got lucky, but most major luck comes with some proper positioning and the experience to get there. Back to that sweet spot for the profit-competitive higher education landscape in the USA. With more than 3,000 colleges and universities in the United States, each one is always trying to stand out. At the time, Rowan University was a couple of years into a major expansion program to double the size of the school and was working to cement a new brand to build an international name, rather than being the local state school. I was inspired to help that vision, as Gina had been when she started ASNE a year and a half before. The namesake of the school, Henry Rowan, who had the school named after him when he gave what was at the time the largest donation to a public school in history, $100 million dollars, was a proud entrepreneur. The founder of the Electrical and Computer Engineering department, Dr. Schmalzel, had always emblazoned in our mind, NALIBO. Always yelled loudly and with passion, for almost any application, even if it didn't really make sense, "Never Accept Limits Imposed By Others" (unlike the study abroad quote I mentioned earlier) was actually emblazoned on the walls of the engineering building. While nobody had actually imposed a limit on sending students to Australia, I imagined one, and I was determined to break it.

We did. After months of hard work and planning, we conducted an application process, and after raising over $30,000 to do so, sent ten students to Australia. I will never forget after that long and formal planning process and all the official budget meetings and funding requests, how the literal first three seconds upon arrival went down. Coming down that escalator in the Townsville, Australia airport with the bright heat of the day seething through the windows in an opulent show of tropical Australian paradise, I saw Ashley in person for the first time. With his hands out and a big smile on his face, he greeted us in true Australian valor, yelling, "Oi Cunts!" To say we were shocked by this tremendously bad word is an understatement.

In the months of planning the trip, we had proceeded with our best go at being incredibly formal to win the hearts and minds of the benefactors supporting the trip and to embed the serious mission we were undergoing. Only once did we have a hint at what we would encounter culturally upon arrival. Having completed multiple internships with US defense contractors, I was aware of the incredibly strict protocols in place for foreign visitors: multiple emails were sent, mounds of paperwork were completed, and giant orange badges labeled anyone from out of country. In Australia, one of our primary agenda items was to make a visit to Lockheed Martin, one of the companies with which I had an internship. Their protocols were more relaxed than required in the USA. The planning call for the visit ahead of the trip was very formal, and upon nearing conclusion, the employees on the other end asked if we required a formal agenda for the trip. We paused, then replied, "No, the notes we've collected during the call should be sufficient," to which we received a reply that bounded out of the phone in jubilation: "EXCELLENT, that's how we rock and roll," and the call ended. So Ashley's surprise should not have caught us as off guard as it did. But it did, and we were in for a culture shock.

Australia has an absolutely raw and untamed environment and culture. It is hard to fathom the fact that a landmass the size of the USA has the mere population of the New York City metropolitan area. We were lucky that James Cook University was in Townsville, a city that was not often regarded as a large tourist hub.

While we toured the absolutely breathtaking, beautiful, magnetic island and had the opportunity to explore the local town and meet incredible people, we compiled a list of more than 100 slang words used by the Australians to describe just about anything you could imagine. I even had the opportunity to hang out with one of the students, Bowie, a self-proclaimed "Bogan" (semi-slang-equivalent to the US term "redneck"), who took us on his motor boat to go wakeboarding in a crocodile and snake infested lake, as he inserted his token word "propa" into every third sentence. "Not to worry," he scoffed when I pointed at the giant warning sign at the boat launch for snakes and crocodiles. "If you see 'em, swim faster."

The trip to Australia was an absolute success. We stayed with students to learn how they lived, shadowed them in their classes to understand how they learned, and visited industry locations to understand how the way they lived and learned affected their workplace culture. We participated in a hands-on, in-nature hackathon that was open to the entire community for a day, funded by the local government, on developing internet of things solutions to study different constructs in nature and how they could be applied in architecture to reduce energy consumption in buildings. We conducted strong meetings with the school's administrative leadership and with the students to pursue a lasting partnership and drive forward the progress. At the height of it all, another university flew students in from Brisbane and we conducted a sumo robot tournament, and I even got on the Australian news.

One of the leaders in the Dean's office, fascinated by my involvement in IEEE, recommended that I attend an upcoming IEEE Congress in Sri Lanka for all of the IEEE volunteers in the Asia-Pacific region.

Our time wrapped in Townsville and we skipped down to Sydney where we toured multiple universities and caught wind of a "State of Origin" thing that was going down. Turns out it was no small thing – it was the equivalent to the US Superbowl for rugby, and it was against a team from the Australian state where Townsville is, Queensland. Naturally, we bought tickets supporting the Maroons from up north and were off to the game. I have never been so harassed at a sporting event. It was a madhouse, and we had the best seats in the house with our thousand or so companion

Queenslander supporters. This event was taking place at the old Olympic stadium and there were 82,000 people in attendance. The lights dimmed, the crowd hushed, and the giant flags took the field, then the dancers, then the drummers, then the end zones lit up. A battle of the bands began, and columns of fire in the colors of each team fired into the electric air. It was undeniably powerful. Queensland took home the win.

We did not. At each leg of the trip, two people were in charge of keeping us on schedule, and in Sydney we missed one of the most important events: a tour of a local broadcasting station with the leaders of IEEE from New South Wales who had provided incredible support in setting up our entire time in Sydney. Somehow cheaper than all of us staying in a hostel was renting a three-story penthouse on Bondi Beach through Airbnb. It was incredible, but it was getting to be too much for me. It was hard to blame my traveling companions – several of our students had never left the United States before in their lives, and they were losing focus of why we were there. They acted like the trip was to party and enjoy themselves. The simple fact was that they could. For the most part, we only had responsibilities about two hours every day, but it was getting out of hand. As lead of the trip, I had a responsibility to make sure that everyone stayed on course, but I remember seeing the looks on several of their faces of purely and absolutely not caring at all. How could this be? How could they not understand the privilege of our situation and the mission we had? Was it possible that this was a failure, had I lost control of everyone, and more importantly, was my overall mission of educating others on the power of other cultures unachievable for individuals who had grown up so siloed from the rest of the world?

I took the elevator down those dozen stories from the penthouse and walked out onto the small patch of grass in front of the building and lay down, trying to get away from it all, frustrated beyond belief. We had literally come so far. Staring up at the stars, it occurred to me how incredibly clear they were, despite being in a large metropolitan area; it made me think of home. I was lying on the exact opposite side of the globe. Reflecting back on that moment, while I did not think it at the time, the trip was not a failure. It was a massive success for the students, who learned an incredible amount.

Upon return, Rowan basked in the publicity; our financial sponsors had gotten what they were looking for. I sat in the Dean's office and read out all of the potential partners for the university, both academic and industry; the options were many. I will never understand why, but even after investing all that money, the Dean chose to pursue none of them. With that decision, the partnership faded, but remained an incredible bookmark in the prominent milestones for globalizing the reach of Rowan University. For the IEEE student branch club, I had delivered. In the end, I doubled the membership of the club and increased the annual recurring budget by 300%, not including the $30,000 for the trip to Australia, and established a long line of leaders who continued the growth of the student branch after I left. It was the "resume-builder" of a lifetime and unleashed a torrent of opportunities on the international stage.

Action Items Related to Chapter Four

1. Attend a stand-up comedy show on a topic you don't find interesting and take note of what the audience finds most outstanding – think from their perspective and identify what drives

the type of humor they are enjoying. Why doesn't it click with you?

2. On a clear night, find five constellations in the sky and read/learn about them. Next time you travel, find them or know why you can't.

3. Take an aside with a group that you are in. School project, work team, or volunteer effort. Ask the team why they are participating in this effort and what type of personal growth are they gaining. Recap the output as a mechanism to brainstorm how you can perform better as a team.

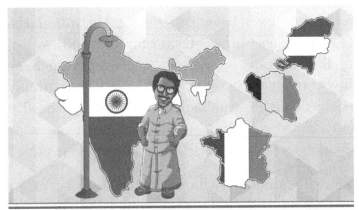

5: OF BORDERS, RELIGION, AND PERCEPTION

Lesson: "The core of man's spirit comes from new experiences." ~ Jon Krakauer, Into the Wild

In this Volatile, Ubiquitous, Complex, and Ambiguous (VUCA) world, everything has already begun or is beginning to stir with the advancement of technology and increasing challenges it brings. The airport itself has transformed from a mere spot comprising of a runway, a couple of hangers, some fuel tanks, and a basic platform for boarding the plane, to a more advanced station of many terminals, gates, high-end waiting rooms, boarding ramps with amazing architecture, and duty-free shops to make a traveler's experience more luxurious and untiring. However, this builds into large travel times between terminals and gates, endless airport queues, and concepts such as layovers and customs. In 2013, I was in my early twenties and hadn't really experienced a cultural shock that could open my eyes wide enough to see the world from a new perspective.

That in mind, the chance to travel to India for an IEEE student and young professional congress was both exciting and startling. What excited me most was finally visiting a country that has strong ancestral roots with the country that I have called my motherland ever since I was born. Imbibed by childhood memories of growing up watching Bollywood movies and India-Pakistan cricket stars, I was exhilarated to solidify my travel plans to beautiful India. Yet, the political conditions and past conflict scenarios had produced tension in everyone's mind, leading me to think twice to travel.

Nevertheless, I had peak anticipation, and it didn't really bother me, knowing that the worst that could potentially happen to the group of boys that I was joining was to make a memorable trip and collect lifelong stories that would forever make me proud. Born Pakistani, I did go a few times to Wahgah, the Pakistan-

India border located on the highway between Lahore (Pakistan) and Amritsar (India). With withering skin and sweat-dripping from our foreheads from the heat of the region, the dreamlike experience you get every time from watching soldiers with their pressed uniforms and flamboyantly colorful headgear marching and displaying extravagant moves, each striving to dominate the other party, with crowds in the background going crazy and chanting nationalistic slogans, leads to an atmosphere of overpowering patriotism. It was always intriguing to think how the world would look standing on that side of the border, looking at the Indian crowd supporting their soldiers – a crowd similar to us, yet different in their performance.

This was the ultimate chance to go to India by pedaling across the border and taking an ever-imaginative picture of standing on one foot in Pakistan and the other in India, the feeling of standing in two countries at the same moment. I didn't want to make this trip go quick by taking an airplane ride; my sole purpose was to experience the whole journey of going into a country that offers culture distinctive to ours, but surely alike to how I was born and raised.

We, the mighty boys, finally made this trip in July, 2013.

We crossed the famous Wahgah Border for the first time ever. I can still remember how I felt. A surge of blood streamed through my body looking at distant Pakistan, the country which made me what I am today, and a sudden thought made me contemplate "What if I don't make it back to Pakistan? What if I am arrested for something, and don't know the reason? What if I don't ever see the people I really love and depend on?" The flood of such "what if" questions gushed through my mind, but it was too late, and who was I to complain? I was the one who wanted to experience everything by foot.

I must admit, those stereotypes and bad things that polluted my nascent mind with enough hatred and fear to consider all Indians particularly responsible for the terrorism issues and the Kashmir dispute stopped when I finally visited India and saw the welcoming nature of people no different than us. The biggest understanding that I developed from this trip is no doubt that Pakistan and India don't get along for reasons that have their legitimate justifications but that only a marginalized group among their humongous population would go and do those evil things. It can be politicians brainwashing the citizens with their demagogue nature to win elections or the diplomatic policies of a few authoritative bureaucrats that are influenced by many external factors. An educated and literate common person is never stupid enough to believe whatever wrong is preached. Surely the uneducated or unaware side of the population (usually in rural parts) might be easy influenced with such chants and non-facts, but that's not just the case with Pakistan and India, but everywhere in the world.

Both countries, when they got their independence from the British back in 1947, were disintegrated into two separate nations, each lying on the foundation of its religion and ethnicity. India was largely populated by people who believed in Hinduism, keeping other religions such as Islam, Christianity, Sikhism, Buddhist, etc., in the minority. Similarly, Pakistan was hugely dominated by Islamic principles, attracting a population that believed in Islam, keeping Hinduism, Christianity, Sikhism, and Zoroastrians as the minority to make a democratic Islamic republic in the region. Well, certainly that's not the case as per my observations and knowledge. Surely as kids we were taught in our schools the reason for the whole sub-continent to divide was religion. Only a few facts can convince anyone to change their mind that, in fact, it was more of a self-belonging and opportunistic mindset that manifested, separating the countries as equally and equitably as contractual agreements can. One of the facts that is hard to digest is the minority of Muslims in India is in fact more than the whole Islamic-based republic of Pakistan. Moreover, Pakistan, mostly in its Sindh province, has a sizeable population of Hindus whose ancestors refused to migrate to India, accepting Pakistan as their homeland. I assume, perhaps, that the same happened in India for Muslims who didn't like the idea of migrating to a country which could offer more religious security and compassion.

What stays the same is the fact that both the countries are rich in culture and patriotic passion. It is also ludicrous to see a region divided into both countries such as Hyderabad City, where Nizams (monarchs) once ruled for centuries, which now share the land that is set apart by a geopolitical boundary. Thus, if you are not from these two countries and you want to visit Hyderabad or have already visited, don't tell anyone that you visited Hyderabad; instead, mention which Hyderabad you went to. This was the among the top reasons for me to make a trip to India, since I went to an engineering college that was in Hyderabad, Pakistan and our final stop-over would be at Hyderabad, India. I wanted to experience the feel of seeing both the Hyderabads and to acquaint myself with the similarities and differences of a city that has the same ancestral background but now different civic and municipal leaders progressing their own agenda and mission.

India is geographically huge. Not as huge as the United States or Russia but comparatively more than Pakistan. The farthest road journey from its southern part to any northern part could take perhaps 24-30 hours of straight road driving. It took around half this time without stopping from Atari (Wahgah Border) to Delhi, the capital of India, from where we headed to Hyderabad on a nearly two hour journey flying from Delhi's Airport. I imagined how much time it would have taken us if we were to road-trip from the border to Hyderabad, and that is not even where India ends, as it extends further south.

We, the boys group, were just out of breath considering the fact that we finally crossed the border into India. This was a dream-like moment for me; our van driver, a middle-aged lower-income citizen entertained us with his commentary throughout the road journey. Leveraging his seniority, we asked all the dos and don'ts to stay safe and not create embarrassing situations.

Delhi is the embodiment of what a metropolitan city should look and be like. The new part is as flamboyant as per its image – students laden with bags, corporates with their suits, and an underground train network make it a new and moderate Delhi. However, it is the old Delhi that astounds. When you walk within the crowded streets, filled with many sideway eateries and traders selling their stuff on kiosks, a flow of thoughts wander through you as you imagine how simplistically beautiful life in old Delhi is. It is the same city as new Delhi, yet different in its approaches, lifestyles, and infrastructure – distinguished as new and old.

I will stop and make a point of emphasis here: No matter how many countries you have been to or how many you are in the process of traveling to, if you don't carry the beauty within yourself, you'll never find it wherever you go. It is the moments that make us take a detailed look at ourselves, it is the cultural archetypes that make you reflect on yourself and your surroundings, in parallel with finding beauty in the personal revelation from the nadirs of disorder in life.

Spending many days in India, I was culturally shocked to see the similarities between India and Pakistan. For example, a huge population is poor and underdeveloped, spending a major part of their lives in the slums. Nonetheless, they still have smiling faces, hearts that could welcome you from their core, and hope for betterment. Maybe that's the reason why any North American or European finds it difficult to comprehend their living situation and unswerving happiness.

Secondly, what's more common is the "Jugaad" – an improvised homemade solution to a problem that is cheap and easy but not reliable in many circumstances. I saw the same drive and thinking for finding Jugaadi solutions in both countries. Jugaad is somehow implanted in our blood streams, from machines, to people, to systems; we are surrounded by Jugaad. While in India during the month of July, the temperature (in the 40s Celsius) brought scorching heat. All the rooms and buildings without roof cover were exposed to direct sunlight, making it warmer than ever. I saw some Indians putting ice cubes on the fan so cold drops circulating around the room would make a difference in the room temperature. I thought: what a Jugaad for not having an air-conditioner. I recall one of my Jugaad from childhood was a desire to have skating boots. Of course, we didn't have flat roads, but I wanted to cross over streets sprinting fast in my boots. By the time my father could have brought me one, I managed to make my own by the Jugaadi solution of using an old rusted shoe binding, its sole adorned with the broken small tires of a rotating office chair, to at least get a feel of how you manage running wearing a boot with a tire.

Third, what's still common in both of us is to never say sorry or thank you in public places; formality, perhaps, is not our strong suit. You can expect to hear nothing after giving away your seat on a bus to an elderly or handicapped person. It's totally common this way. We don't usually greet shopkeepers whenever we visit them; we get straight to the point and save our precious time and words for a future time and moment that might possibly never come, until we realize we should be saying these formal words. To an honest end, I did experience the same attitude in India, and it didn't surprise me or the rest of the group, but it did to one of our Japanese friends who joined us for a stroll in the city once, asking us whether the recipient of his gratitude wasn't understood in English or if they were too stupid to at least say thanks? We assured him this is fine, it is just how we people are, and not to take it seriously.

Although many of the similarities didn't surprise us, there were few instances which literally flustered our minds. One of them was the head-nod for signaling trivial emotions such as yes and no. In Pakistan, and generally around the world, you nod up and down to signal you agree or simply wanted to mean "yes", and the head-nod right and left means "no". But that was different in India: you tip your head and nod right and left to actually mean "yes", but that was not exactly the same nod, it was more of a head tilt completely to one side and spring it on both sides to the other end, expressing you actually wanted to disagree. For instance, we were once not exactly sure if we were on the correct path toward our destination, and we asked a local. He made that spring-loaded to-and-fro nod and (while we had understood he wanted to say no) he uttered yes, you are headed in the right direction. To be honest, we all were baffled at this situation, so we confirmed again by just showing our hand to one direction and asking, "This is the right way, right?" He nodded again, and we were like, "No brother, you say something, but you nod different." We thought he was crazy or making a fool of us, so we (of course) didn't thank him and asked another person. To our surprise he nodded the same and he agreed with us. That moment we looked at each other and all got the gist that this nod is an agreement over here.

Another time, we spoke in the Hindi language, considering it as the national language, but people didn't respond back. I remember one also mocked us, inquiring why we were not speaking English. We thought to say, "Because Hindi is your national language, and if you can't speak that, don't expect us to speak English." Later, we got to know that India doesn't have a national language, rather regional languages. Though Pakistan has many cultures residing within its boundaries, each speaking a different language and fostering diverse values, the Urdu language continues to be its nationally-spoken language, with the Punjabi dialect as the most spoken language in Pakistan.

This trip exposed me to many avenues of cultural shifts, only a few of which I will be able to write here in this chapter. I will first describe how I felt sharing my room with an Indian himself. The congress in Hyderabad was organized by local members of IEEE in Hyderabad and gathered students and young professionals from all over Asia and the Pacific. Apart from many activities planned, one of the purposes for these sorts of congresses is to instill a sense of globalization among participants. Before that event, I had never shared a room with an Indian. Though I did have chances to talk and interact, sleeping and sharing your space with an Indian in a four-cornered arrangement was never my cup of tea.

My new friend Siddi Jai was an engineer, like myself, and was – all things considered – a great human. His greatness manifested itself through his viewpoints and behavior. We spent almost every night talking about our stuff, answering each other's religious and political questions. We tried to maintain a respect and integrity for each other's beliefs, but took the great opportunity to discuss in length our existing beliefs and reasons to think this way. I once wanted to pray inside the room, and so considering Hyderabad, I knew I could find a prayer mat easily through the reception desk, and I did, in fact. When I returned, Siddi was there ready to perhaps work on his computer. I thought first to quit my plan – not because he was Indian but because I didn't know how he would feel watching me pray namaz (Salah) being a Hindu himself. He was mature enough to let me know that he wouldn't care and would even go to the hotel lobby until I prayed as much as I could if that's what I wanted him to do. Surely, I didn't bother him much and prayed in the room.

On another night we had a gala arranged by the organizers to mingle with everyone and to interact informally. It started with an act that, little did I know at the time, was a way to depict Hindu Lord Ganesh's life. I watched as if it were a regular unique performance. Later on, Siddi shared with me the whole plot and backstory of Lord Ganesh, and I must admit, as much as I was enthusiastic to learn from a person who believed in the faith, I was also pleased realizing that nothing bad happened, that nothing felt strange after taking in a story about Hindu Gods and their history.

Infested in my mind by a local madrasa (Islamic religious seminary) when I was a kid, the concept of believing in our God meant disagreeing with everything else to prove our love and affection to the Almighty. That alone meant agreeing to not even discuss anything related to other religions because this can lead to committing "Kufr – a sin that can haunt my life". It is with confidence that I can attest not all madrassas are equal and not all preach hatred and animosity, but I was unlucky; I went to the wrong one. Even my parents realized something developing – and wrong through my changed behavior. Talking to Siddi, I realized how for-granted about Islam I have been throughout my whole life and how I never challenged my learnings or questioned existing faiths with questions. The vague and unappropriated answers that I gave to Siddi's Islamic questions were enough of an eye-opener for me to study Islam once again – perhaps the right way. This was possible when I studied the Holy Book by understanding its contexts and by openly discussing them with the world. What followed were days filled with joy and nights that sparkled with life.

The time in Hyderabad quickly wrapped up, and it was time to get back to Pakistan. We did, however, visit the Char-Minar, an architecture with four minarets built in the 15th century by Mughals with a mosque on top.

Little did we know there was more to come that could get us a once in a lifetime experience of fear, terror, and entrapment before we could depart the monumental India. Delhi, the same city that gave us chills when we arrived a few days ago to board a flight to Hyderabad, soon became a point of terror when one of our colleagues (who didn't have anything with him in his pockets, including cash and his passport at the time it happened) suddenly went missing. Rajiv Chowk is an intersection of the metro train network and one of the busiest stops serving the famous Connaught Place (a high-end shopping plaza). It is always crowded with people from Delhi. While boarding the train, Rahul, one of the boys with us, somehow lost hold of us and was taken aback in this rush. At first, we didn't take it seriously, but it haunted us when he didn't come and wasn't seen anywhere for the next 2-3 hours.

What followed next was frustration and havoc among us. We had a train to catch at night, which was to take us to Amritsar city to depart via the Wahgah border early the next morning, since our visa was expiring within the next 30 hours or so. We spent the next few hours looking for Rahul in all train, bus, and public stations, but he was nowhere to be found. He didn't have money nor his passport. This particularly worried us for two reasons. One, without a passport, he had symbolically no identity in India and no one would have believed him if he were not able to show his ID upon request by any police or official. Two, India's visa required us to arrive together and depart together, so without him, the remaining five of us couldn't cross the border.

Even writing this now, I am getting chills in my body, and I can't fully tell how I felt at that time with this situation that could lead to any number of worse situations. Whenever I tell anyone this story, the next moment they ask, "Why didn't you go to the police directly and seek their help instead of your own efforts in finding him?" I don't blame you for thinking this way; every normal person would say that for sure. But what restricted us was our own mistake, and in fact I must say a huge blunder that we had just made in our lives. India's visa for Pakistanis is limited to cities – getting a visa doesn't give you access to travel freely. In our case, we got visas only for Hyderabad, which allowed us to transit cities and areas falling in the direction of our destination. Staying in any other city besides Hyderabad for more than 24 hours was a crime. What we were doing in Delhi was actually staying, although we didn't have plans to stay overnight. We had arrived early morning and we were ready to leave by night, but even those recreational trips that we made to explore Delhi were not permitted by our visas. But, as I mentioned earlier, we Pakistanis are true Jugaadis, and we like to break the rules. We are very much accentuated with the idea of "my life, my rules".

Now, get a new perspective of thinking: try to visualize yourself in this situation, where you are not permitted to visit Delhi, but you did. One of your friends went missing and doesn't have a passport with him. You have a train to take that night, but you can't leave even if you want to since you can only cross the border all together, and finally you are afraid to go to the police since this will let them ask first, "What are you doing in Delhi in the first place?" When we realized we would have to act mature, even though some of us did cry and were already swamped with bad and evil thoughts, we decided to cancel the train tickets when time was near and to approach police before we could change our minds.

We went to the police and we told them everything. The police, as depicted in Bollywood movies, started with regular abuses and threats (don't mind, even Pakistani police might have done the same if any Indian group would had been in this situation). They made us shit our pants when one of them yelled at us "that we will rot in jail forever", but thankfully the police found Rahul and they let us go after we apologized, making promises to never do the same again in our lives.

We were amazed how the Indian police let us go, just like that. I must credit Inam Bhutto, one of our colleagues who claimed he used to be a top debater and comrade in undergrad times. His stubbornness and confidence allowed him to deal with this situation like an adult. He was surely the one among us that stayed motivated and proved to us he was a comrade. My acting skills did a little work – I cried and delivered as emotional a dialogue as I could to develop sympathy with the police. We still don't know what worked, but at least we were relieved that we were again free men.

We rented a van and drove all night, risking our lives and without any stop, reaching the Wahgah border early in the morning to depart for our homeland after this restless torture. We didn't talk much throughout our journey; that experience was enough to make us cherish our lives and value our citizenship. We were welcomed to Pakistan with our parents' and professors' calls scolding us one by one on how insane we were to think of making this blunder. This was 2013, but it still haunts me whenever I recall that moment. I was a changed man when I came back.

I once read a quote in a book that summarized the essence of traveling by deliberating on the thought that cities are always like people. A city shows its personality to the traveler, its challenges and emotions. It can reflect a mutual love, care, or friendship if the traveler connects with its offerings; however, just like people, cities too can show hatred. Yet one is liable to never truly understand a city's life force without traveling there. That is when you can know where you belong, where are you loved, and where you are excluded. As a traveler, I have had experiences where I have been loved, cared for, or even rejected. That all made me realize that knowing yourself and where you belong rationally is better known when you travel quite often. After an immersive experience of India, the next in line for me was Europe.

An event called the IEEE Sections Congress is like a soccer World Cup, happening once every 3 years and gathering mutually interested IEEE leadership to one location on the globe. Amsterdam, Netherlands was where the Sections Congress was hosted in August, 2014. I fell in love immediately with everything. For sure, why wouldn't I when it's The Amsterdam, The Sections Congress, and perhaps The chance for me at that moment to go and introduce the world to my existence?

I was selected as Secondary Delegate to represent Pakistan at large, and my traveling and hotel expenses were promised to be reimbursed by IEEE. But, perhaps when God wants to test your will, He orders nature to resist until you are no longer afraid of losing and being dejected. I must say, I was afraid and I feared rejection, but that didn't stop me for applying for the visa.

Before I could hear the verdict from the Netherlands Embassy, I excitedly made all the decorative plans of what I was going to do for the rest of the time before my soon-to-be-issued Schengen visa would expire. Yet, before I could drum up more in my imagination, I received a call with bad news. My visa was rejected because they thought I would not come back. Based on past notorious Pakistani travelers, I can't blame them, but it is sad that it has generalized their visa process. Even people like me, who love their country to the fullest, would be seen the same among those that haven't been loyal to Pakistan and were basically cowards to run away from their situations, slipping off into developed countries.

Since I was new to the field of entrepreneurship, traveling for business, and definitely intimate relationships, rejection was not something that I was very accustomed with and I had a fear for everything that could happen worse. I was not prepared to handle or anticipate what lay beyond these rejections for me. That night, I feel no shame in admitting, I cried.

I had cried a few months before when my application for the Social Innovation in Digital Context program was selected as a semi-finalist and even interviewed for a full-time fellowship opportunity in Sweden at its conclusion. I couldn't imagine exactly what, but I knew something would surely come up where I would be traveling to Europe, and the Sections Congress was that chance. But then with the rejection of my visa, the chances looked slim. I regrouped myself the next morning.

Nevertheless, I must say that over the years, if there's one skill that involves emotions where I have continually progressed, it is forgetting the past and regaining motivation for the future. Besides, that was one of those days where I had done the unthinkable: re-apply for the visa with more clear documents and written justification. The days passed by, but I did not hear back. Suddenly, one day I got a call, and again my visa application was rejected.

I don't know how to put this into words, but with only a week left until the Sections Congress, the chances of getting a visa straight on the third attempt were slim, but it didn't bother me much at all. I still applied with a final hope that the decision might change for the better. It was 19th August, 2014 when I got a call in the afternoon from a drop box office number that they have received my passport and I should come hurry as quick as I can, since they would be closing in an hour. I didn't have tomorrow because the 20th August was when I was supposed to travel to attend the Sections Congress, which was starting the day after in Amsterdam. I rushed and drove as fast as I could on my motorbike, arriving to see that I finally got the Schengen visa on my third attempt – I was free to go to Europe!

My tenacious regular attempts at the visa application made me achieve success, even after my travel agent had given his honest opinion, after my second attempt, that I would only be wasting my time and another few thousand Pakistani rupees on a third try. I had already spent so many thousands of rupees and a significant portion of my time, so nothing was more logical than for me to apply as much as I could, until I was sure the last available plane that could have flown me to Amsterdam was off the ground. I thought to take one more chance; my subconscious mind kept reminding me, "You don't have to stop, it doesn't suit you – the decision surely will come from the Embassy," and I knew the opportunity was still in my hands.

The night before my travel, I didn't sleep due to excitement and pondered over what I already knew about Amsterdam. I have been a great follower of art. From his marvelous work and paintings, Vincent Van Gogh left a legacy that goes beyond words, thoughts, and perhaps, art itself. For someone like me, I always knew the

Netherlands only as the land of the great Vincent Van Gogh, even though I never knew how to pronounce his name, and due to my sluggishness, I never even made a serious attempt to research it on the internet. That night when I decided to research, I was thrilled (basically stunned) to learn of places like De Wallen, the largest and most famous red area district in the world, is in Amsterdam. And little did I know that the same Netherlands, where I had dreams of walking across streets to feel the perspiration in the air for Van Gogh, was the largest exporter of beer in the whole world.

After about 20-22 hours of total journey, I arrived at Schiphol Airport in Amsterdam at night and got out from immigration to experience the chill weather that I was not accustomed to endure. I took a lift from a police guy who was patrolling the streets on his bicycle, and he found me baffled with the mesmerizing beauty of the city and, powered by my insatiable surprise, my luck of finally making it there. What followed after a brief conversation was: he asked me to sit back and tow my carry-bag on its pedaling tires as gently as I could since there wasn't any space where I could put it. As slowly as he could, he rode to leave me exactly at my hotel with some tips.

Included, you ask? Yes, tips from him regarding how and why I should taste different beers in Amsterdam.

Even though I was awake for the last 40 or more hours and had barely slept on my flights, the excitement took hold of me and the adrenaline rush in my body kept me awake the whole night. I was not working, talking, or doing anything important, but the mere thought of getting this far was so powerful that I never felt tired, disgusted, or jet lagged. The night passed by quickly, and the sun rose with a new day. It was a literal new day for me to go out on the streets and finally to the RAI Convention Center where I would meet the top leaders of science, technology, computing, and engineering all in one place at the Sections Congress. With formal and not-so-formal greetings, I made it through two meetings and workshops for the day and quickly made friends with two Sri Lankans who, in the future, would make me believe in serendipity.

The group of us – the two guys from Sri Lanka and I – went out together that night to stroll the streets and at least have an immersive experience on what the world of international sex and dealing at brothels was like. So we headed to the Red Street. To be more modest in my writings here, I felt like someone who had spent all their life watching women wearing bikinis (or not) showcase dance moves to seduce the visitors – but only in movies, dramas, and to some extent Grand Theft Auto video games. Yet, when I saw all that from that near distance and experienced the surreal moments that I had thought about sometimes, I felt relieved. Rest assured that this is not exactly who I am and I should not become so crazy about it. The curiosity of watching a woman with less clothing than required (or accepted) in any developed society soon triumphed.

To some extent, we also wanted to experience a conversation with a prostitute, so we approached a few and acted as if we were pro and have been doing all this for years. The conversations would have started with little cheesy dialogues, followed by romantic flattery, and concluded with details on how much we were willing to spend for what services. I did talk to two and knowing all the details, I thanked them for their time and told them that only excitement had brought me to talk to them.

Wandering through the streets of Amsterdam, I looked for halal food or simply a Desi restaurant (a local indigenous one), but within that I explored some of the dishes that Dutch people make best and are an integral part of their culture. Hagelslag is the one that fascinated my taste, and I later came to know that most of the Dutch population take this buttery bread slice with an abundant coat of hagelslag. What's best was they were normal-like sprinkles but were weightier and flavorful. Besides, I had never thought the combo of bread, butter, and sprinkles would make such a delight. The baker that I visited to buy this every morning told me that she read somewhere that around 700,000 pieces of such buttery bread are eaten every day across the Netherlands, and that seemed true because I saw the bread in many people's hands, and moreover the rush and line for getting a slice of hagelslag spoke for itself.

One day when I arrived at the bakery in the morning to take my hagelslag, Amber, the bakery lady, was putting something in the tray that got my attention and curiosity to ask her, "What is that beautiful thing?" She said in her not-so-good English that this is a lapis legit. To be honest, I didn't catch how she pronounced that, but when I searched the internet, I came to know its history. It is not only Dutch, but a combo of Dutch and Indonesian food and spices.

It is a dessert that normally has 20-30 layers of individually baked cakes in different colors so it looks beautiful, as if you are going to eat a rainbow cake. I am not a food expert so the only taste that I recalled was of egg yolk and spicy butter. I didn't know what more was inside it, but it surely was more than just egg and butter.

At first, I was excited to try it, but Amber said that it's expensive and since I have been a great guest to her and she liked my hairstyle (I seriously don't know what she liked in it), she gave me a discount and encouraged me to try it, and so I did. After knowing the lapis legit history, I was amazed how two different cultures had amalgamated to produce something so tasty. To me, perhaps, this was the best and logical reason for colonists from the Netherlands to make Indonesia a colony, previously called the Dutch Indies in the 15th century. Though the Dutch had departed so long back, this fusion of sweets and spices tell much more about the innovative systems of Dutch colonists and the local people.

Ultimately, Amsterdam is one of my favorite cities in Europe. Though I have traveled to just 8 or 10 cities in different countries, Amsterdam was on top, and if I ever have to migrate to

Europe to live with my family, I would always pick Amsterdam. The beautiful scenery, the nature-filled parks, and the bicycle ecosystem are what make Amsterdam a happier, more beautiful, and less polluted city than many others in the world.

Riding a bike has always been my favorite hobby as kid, but in Pakistan you must either be very poor or very fitness-oriented to ride it with grace on streets where no one would judge you. For sure I don't care what people think about me, but I live within surroundings where there are hundreds of them, so becoming an outlier has its own sacrifices involving judgmental taunts by people, rebelling against society and sometimes being a lunatic in some people's opinions. We also don't have good roads and infrastructure to ride bicycles.

In Amsterdam, from kids to senior citizens, I saw a huge population riding bicycles and decided that instead of spending on trams or trains for local travel, I would go and rent a bicycle and do the thing that I always wished to do – see the major part of a city by riding a bicycle. Very soon I picked up the pace of other bicyclers, and every day I bicycled no less than 6-8 hours, even at night, to see as much as I could. It was a cultural shift to see that those who have pedals have more power on roads and turnabouts, and for the very first time in many years, I felt like a child again, pursuing my journey toward happiness on my bicycle with no one to stop me from imagining the possibilities. According to one research report, Amsterdam is so bicycle-friendly that it has more bicycles than humans living in it, and there were different varieties of bicycle for various purposes. "It's good, isn't it?" said our driver on our last day, directing his hand at a kid's tricycle next to a canal cruise entrance.

As hard as I tried, there was no escape from the deluxe décor of scenes around me. Above, the blue sky and dreamy songs of the supernatural humming of birds; underneath, the sparkling sea called me to unite with an ingenious array of thoughts, speaking the legend of Amsterdam and its historic feats. The unreal experiences in such a dreamlike city like Amsterdam soon came to its conclusion, and we set off on our next journey – to visit Paris, France. Jostling between crowds, we somehow got a ticket on a cheap bus service that would take us via highway to Brussels, Belgium and then to Paris, France.

We had a quick stopover in Brussels. What intrigued me was the fact that you had to pay to pee, and you needed to have the right change of coins and bills. It was not a surprise to me; Pakistan is a country where some public toilets still charge amounts categorizing your in-toilet activities as big and small. Small is when you take a leak (like a quick one) and big is when you do the whole defecation. When I was a kid, I always wondered how they would know what I did inside, so I could lie that I did small and instead do big to save money. Once, I did ask the doorkeeper, and he said they have experience to tell them which it was. For a very brief amount of years, I did try to fool them, saying I was going to take a small but instead did big and sometimes they did catch me telling the lie, but a few times nobody bothered and believed me. I still am clueless with this mystery, so I again thought, "how would the Belgians recognize what's what and how much to charge?" So, I tried lying when I entered, saying that I needed to take a quick leak, and I did take some time since I was doing the big one. When I got out, he asked me to pay a full amount for big, and I tried to negotiate that I did the small one very slowly and that it was habitual for me to take time. He reluctantly said that I had to pay for a big one – it didn't matter if I did small or big, they charged me for my time. To be honest, this answer made sense, more than the Pakistani guy who told me that they have experience. Imagine how it would look if, say, they apply for a position at large toilet facility and their resume says, "I have enough experience to look at a victim's face and tell if they did big or small." They would get the job right away. Pure talent, I guess.

Anyway, before the Belgians kill me for portraying their country as a toilet-charger, we did find time to explore some nearby parks, and one of the greatest things that excited me at that time was a bicycle ride that could charge your cell phone and batteries. It is an intelligent design to encourage cycling while charging your electronic batteries at the same time. Belgium is also famous for chocolates, and this is what we bought for sure. Since time was short and our bus was about to leave for its last stop in Paris, we departed Belgium promising ourselves that we would seek the full Brussels experience next time. For sure the electronic dance music festival "Tomorrowland" is what Belgium is becoming famous for in recent years. It is the world's biggest, and I am seriously planning on attending in the near future.

Before arriving in Paris, I asked to meet up with one of my friends, Pierre, who at that time was a telecommunications engineer by profession but also a part-time food critic living in Paris. Luckily, I got to meet him in Amsterdam at an IEEE Sections conference, since Pierre was an IEEE member. His advice when I asked the best way to spend four days in Paris, was only four words: "eat and make love". Pierre was a regular contributor to the food section of a local newspaper and became my guide in his city of Paris. Yet the very best thing about him was not what I mentioned above, but the fact that he wanted to be a stand-up comedian. To some extent, I also had similar dreams when I was growing up at my high school. The funny incidents about his childhood and youth love stories made me laugh until I got a bulge in my throat, and I started feeling like a senseless fool being sentimental for someone else's childhood.

One evening while in Paris, he showed me around his neighborhood, and I made the Pakistani Karak Chai cup of tea. He said he had never tasted such delight in tea. He said the point is when you are in Paris, to look for a great patisserie, and since I would be a tourist, I might not find intricate differences between patisseries. Every patisserie is not created equal. A patisserie is a French bakery with a lot of sweets and pastry offerings. I started roaming around the streets of Paris looking for the great patisserie but quickly realized Pierre was right when he said that you have to be a local to understand which patisserie offers the best deals in town. He did give me a simple hint: if there are long lines in the morning outside of a patisserie, that means it's simply great.

Overall, Paris was way beyond my expectations, both positive and negative. Within a series of graffiti-strewn walls and artistic buildings, it exposed more than just architectural prettiness but also artfully settled photographic pieces.

I started my day with a croissant and coffee daily, but my chai addiction was killing me; I needed to find a patisserie that could offer me a cup to quench my addiction. Once, I decided I would go and ask the serving lady to kindly give me some milk or a flavor to add in a cup of black brew coffee. Little did I know that this would turn into an embarrassing moment for me. The French mademoiselle who was busy cleaning the counter saw me coming towards her and greeted me, "Bonjour," to which I also tried hard to respond back in a French tone, "Bonjour." At first, I spoke English and asked her if they have milk. She seemed to not understand but still made her way to the bottom of the counter and offered me some sugar cubes. I decided that it was the English causing my troubles, so I pointed with my hands.

However milk might be explained, I was trying it, and it felt like a dumb charades game where my final task was to tell someone with my hands "the milk, the milk please!" She didn't understand at all. The more I gave her hints, the more she showed various eatery and cutlery items. Finally, I saw a hope in the television where a French advertisement for milk was being displayed, and the advertisement plot was scripted between a mother, who was young, beautiful, and elegant, and her infant son. I pointed my hands to the TV and asked her, "This is what I want from you now." She nodded in affirmative and came close as if telling a secret, "Monsieur, you girls, you come at night after 10, girls everywhere here." With a great laughter on my face and a feeling of shyness, I tried to correct her that I was not pointing at that young and beautiful mother, nor the girls which she mentioned, but instead to what she was holding in her hands – the milk. After a round of embarrassment, she finally said, "Ahh, you want du lait," and I said, "Yeah, some Dulle please," and this is how I got a cup of milk coffee in Paris.

Pierre, my friend who was in contact with me all the time, suggested that I should take a sandwich from those patisseries for lunch, as it would come cheap. And to ask for a Coke with it, which very much annoys the French when you eat this way. I didn't actually do this since it seemed disrespectful instead of fun.

Evenings in Paris were beautiful. Firstly, the romantic couples you can see all around urban parts of the city and their intimate caressing made me feel like a loser and put me in the mood to go get a girl, but soon my pride of being strong prevailed, and I concentrated more on the background. But I still sometimes couldn't resist watching that all happening in front of me. Secondly, I ate like a king, with each morning at a patisserie buying croissants and bread and butter, giving me freedom to eat much more than my regular appetite as if there was no tomorrow. Luckily, tomorrow certainly came, and I got to start all over again, ignoring lessons learned from yesterday's experience.

One evening, I met an expat friend for supper, and we chatted over a coffee and cake while sitting shoulder to shoulder on bistro chairs, reflecting on experiences. Suddenly, my inner Satan felt an urge to ask her to be my girl, since for the last two days all I could see were couples together. After all, I did introduce myself well to her, so the chances were strong, but I decided not to take it up to a level where I would depart back to Pakistan saying, "From Paris with Love."

But here's the thing – not only did I become infatuated with the city's patisseries and romance but also with the citizens themselves, as everyone in Paris wandered the walkways gracefully draped in cashmere scarves and fashionable jackets. A whirlwind of emotions occurred when I saw the Eiffel Tower from a very near distance. I took as many pictures as I could and even went up to the top of it. The best thing I saw at the Eiffel Tower was not only couples coming to take pictures kissing each other with the tower in the background, but also newly-married couples all dressed up to capture their best moments with the glorious Eiffel.

Again, a sudden rush of thoughts made me melancholy for a bit, realizing I have nobody to take kissing pictures with, or even to enjoy the evening with. Suddenly, a girl approached me and in her sweet voice asked, "Excuse me sir, would you please take a picture for both of us?" For one moment I thought she was alone and by "both" she meant me and her. Before I could thank God for listening to my wish, a boy came over and started to kiss her while I stood there dumbly thinking, "What is happening?" She halted in the middle and directed with her hands to take a picture while they are kissing and to make sure I got a good complete view of the Eiffel Tower behind them.

I must say that at this particular moment, I felt like a complete loser, but for sure I captured their moment. They thanked me a lot afterwards, and I went over again to Pierre that night to ask him if he could help me hook up with some French girl. Pierre, as funny as he could be, asked me, "What would you like to do with a French girl?" I told him that the only two things that I knew already about the French were: "French fries and French kiss", so I was good with either one if given with love. Alas, it was not to be.

Coincidentally, my professor from Pakistan also took a trip to Paris with his wife at the same time. I saw it from his Facebook posts. So, the next day, my professor again joined me, and we went to see the Champs-Elysees, Arc de

Triomphe, and the famous Louvre Museum to see the world-renowned Mona Lisa painting. While I tried to see as much as I could in Paris, there was still so much left over to see for next time.

Yet, like a grandeur lightning strike from the Eiffel Tower, I felt like it was time for a change; maybe not a complete one, but an artificial change for sure. I would try to work on my appearance and change my state of mind. I felt like those little talks at patisseries, watching over the denizens of the city, and watching people enjoy life with as small a thing as a good croissant breakfast, started right away to change me. I invested in a cashmere sweater in an indigo color that perhaps I would have never thought to wear in Pakistan. It cost me around 150 euros. Immediately, it felt like a million rupees wasted, but that investment was worth it. Whenever I wear my indigo color sweater, I do get whistles and comments from people around.

Later, I had a long layover in the Charles de Gaulle Airport in Paris and reflected on my memories and moments from Paris. I had a minor awakening due to travel, and I contemplated what had intrigued me most in

Paris: its beauty, the fashion sense of the people, or its nature. I grasped that it was more the interactions I had with people like Pierre, the patisserie lady, and the romantic girl who asked me to take pictures. Pierre might have thought he was just sharing some wise advice on how to have the best time in Paris, but in the end, he – along with those memories from Dehli and Amsterdam – helped me to see a better me.

Action Items Related to Chapter Five

1. Research regulated sex trade and its impact for everyone involved. Then research human trafficking in your locale - understand its presence and simple ways to combat it.

2. Go to a nice restaurant you have never been to and enjoy a meal alone – reflect on what you naturally come to think about during your time there.

3. Host a dinner/lunch party for minimum of five guests with three courses. From meal preparation to determining the guest list to driving the conversation, what did you socially do and not do intentionally

or unintentionally during the evening?

Part Two

After the Elevator

"It's kind of fun to do the impossible."

~Walt Disney

Jeffrey Eker Jr. & Sarang Shaikh

6: EARTH'S SUPERFICIAL DESERT UTOPIA

Lesson: "If opportunity doesn't knock, build a door." ~ Milton Berle

Dubai, and generally the whole United Arab Emirates, serves as a good monument to the philosophical aura and framework that allow us to appreciate the various facets of life. The notion of "the more you understand, the less you know" seems perfect when Dubai is considered as a case study. The city has everything for almost every social class. You see, I mentioned "every class", and this is where Dubai's big and brash, flamboyant, and opulent class distinguishes itself from its small, poor, labor, and penniless class. The variance ranges from ground to sky, and for anyone having a socialist mindset, this concept of having lifestyles from poor as hell to rich at the top seems unreasonable to humanity. But on the flip side, it offers a lot to capitalists and to those who want to double their investment as quickly as possible. People, no matter how rich or poor, have considered Dubai as their ultimate destination. A tourist type wishes to come to see its dwellings and offerings, which are built on the blood and money of a cross-section of society that sees Dubai as a greater source of income for them and their families.

The more you see of Dubai, I suppose, the less you understand it. It's an epistemological dilemma, since what you see, or should I say, see what you are shown, is far beyond what your eyes and mind can predict. Just beyond your vision is the darker side of those construction workers, waiters, and lower working class, carried from their work sites to a big wasteland and poor neighborhood a distance from the city, where they are quarantined away at the end of the workday.

There's a famous joke about expats residing in Dubai, which lightheartedly summarizes the concept of living and working in the city. It starts with a question asked from a worker in

Dubai. "Where do you live? – I live in Dubai. No, this is what you tell your family and friends, but in which specific city do you actually live? – Oh, you mean where I live specifically? It's Sharjah." Nevertheless, it's a cultural pot where you will probably see fewer locals on the streets and more travelers and expats. Dubai offers a good experience if you are into learning different cultures.

It is hard for me to understand why someone who has traveled to a lot of Asia and the Middle East has not yet seen Dubai. At a minimum, nearly every flight goes through to take a stopover in Dubai, and a visa is pretty easy to acquire for a few days to hang around. My first encounter in Dubai happened when I traveled with my family to Saudi Arabia. We had a connecting flight to take from Dubai Airport, and I still remember how dumbfoundedly surprised I was looking at the gigantic size of the airport. It took us more than an hour to walk from one end to other, snap pictures, do some window shopping, and try out some food. Though it was just a layover, I knew that someday I would come back and spend more days visiting the city and not just the airport.

My father, who went to Dubai in the early 1980s and shared his experiences while in flight for Saudi Arabia, had heard that Dubai was a land of opportunity. This was even the case in the 1980s when there was literally nothing in the city except Hyatt Hotels and the Deira Gold Market.

To my amazement, I learned as I returned back to Pakistan that one of my dearest friends, who happened to be a lot older and a senior to me, had settled in Dubai. While he was lost but not forgotten, it was thanks to Facebook, where I had uploaded some of my pictures, that a mutual friend made the e-reintroduction to my old friend, Faraz.

While I never had an elder brother, this friend lived in my neighborhood, and as a kid was pretty much the one to whom I always looked for help and guidance. He repaired my computers for free; he helped me get good video game CDs; and he helped me get into street cricket teams when they typically shooed me away. Moreover, he helped save me from bullies around the neighborhood. As he graduated from high school, Faraz got a technical diploma in telecommunications, as did many in the early

2000s, as Pakistan was surging through a telecom boom.

My motivation to get a telecommunications engineering degree came from Faraz, since we all admired his efforts and my father was a great supporter of his work. Since he made a good deal of money in Dubai after studying telecom, I thought I would do the same and this would be my reason to settle in Dubai in the future. My graduation came with news that was certainly good for all of us. I got a job in one of the leading telecommunications companies in Pakistan, and I started talking to Faraz on social media about my chances to get a job in Dubai.

In 2014, I got the chance for the first time to travel to Dubai for training. It got me excited, since now I could meet Faraz and see the Dubai life. I stayed at one of the more magnificent and wealthier hotels of the city. Everything was so made up, and the size of my room astonished me, as before I never would have stayed in such a large-sized room with a mighty king-sized bed. Everything was so attractive: the room, the view of skyscrapers from the window, and even the bathroom for its technology.

The hotel was owned by a family of Indian origin, probably from the southern side, and the owners were so down-to-earth that they wore a dhoti, a long loincloth wrapped around the hips and thighs, traditionally worn by South Indians. To my utter disappointment, the hotel staff didn't wear black suits (as the hotel uniforms usually are), but rather a blue suit with a red tie. This was bad news for me, since I brought one suit and that was blue with a red tie. To look a bit different, I changed my tie to blue and sometimes didn't wear the jacket to distinguish myself from the hotel staff.

But there was a day when my professor and I decided to go around and visit the Jumeira Beach. We were told by the concierge that the hotel offered one free limousine ride to those who have come to Dubai for the first time, just as a courtesy to make them feel welcome. We arranged a pick-up, moved out to the entrance, and waited.

The hotel had a lot of their staff from India: the gatekeeper was an Indian Sikh, the ladies at reception were beautiful Indian teenagers, and I even had the opportunity to meet one of the chefs, a Hyderabadi Muslim Indian. We thought maybe the driver would be an Indian, too. Per our assumption, we saw one Indian-dressed guy wearing dhoti and a white colored shirt constantly looking at us, and to be specific, me directly. He was standing as if he were waiting for someone, and he held up his phone a few times to perhaps call someone to inquire. I thought maybe this was the guy who was going to drive us and he didn't know he was here to pick us up. Besides, his stares annoyed me, so I went up to him and asked, "Sir, are you my driver?" His face turned red and his expression changed to surprise, and after gasping for a few seconds he said, "No, I am one of the owners of this hotel." I was embarrassed at that moment, but my curiosity got ahold of me and I asked him, "Sorry, but why were you looking at me, then?" He said, "Because, with your blue suit, I thought you were my driver."

Dubai offers a lot, and it's pretty much possible to travel on a budget. As I said earlier, it has everything for every social class. So, if you are low on budget, you can take a stay in the suburbs of Deira, one of the oldest and cheapest neighborhoods of Dubai, wrangle at markets and eat desi food from either a Pakistani or Indian café. Due to the huge influx of population from South Asian countries, the food will be found cheap, and I always found it to be exactly the equivalent price of what I was paying in Pakistan. You can roam around almost all major tourist sites on the metro train, which comes cheap, though some of them are a fair distance from the city. For those you might consider taking a taxi.

In Dubai, everything seems like a world-record breaker, so after a while you will be accustomed to hearing something is the biggest/tallest/fastest/coolest space or area in the world. The sheer size of the Dubai Mall and others would amaze anyone who is traveling for the first time. It is not quite possible to shop and see the whole mall in just a day. Nope, not possible. I remember that when I first traveled to the Dubai Mall I was speechless. How could a shopping mall be so big that inside of it the polo-type taxi runs inside to take you to your favorite outlet or corner? Being the flabbergasted guest, I was walking in the middle of a walkway at the Dubai Mall and suddenly I heard "beep", as if a vehicle were honking its horn to my back. I considering ignoring it: how could a vehicle come inside the mall? I thought it must be someone's mobile ringtone or music. But when it got to be too much, I looked back and the polo-taxi driver directed with his hands for me to take a side. I did and also saw him passing by while cursing me for my ignorance.

One of the major attractions that I really wanted to visit was the top of Burj Khalifa. Imagine how perfect that would sound: "I have been to the tallest building in the world" – that sure seemed like a personal record-breaker and bucket-list item fulfillment. The almost 830-meters-tall Khalifa tower was the world's tallest building until now. The view from the observation deck up on the 148th floor is mind boggling. Nothing appears to be real; the architecture that once looked so big and huge to you when you saw it on the road looks too small to believe. From that height, everything looks like a child's miniature of the world. Sure, going to the top is not cheap, but it is totally worth it if you are into that stuff. But again, everything is a record-breaker so a usual journey for someone who doesn't have their own car and is taking the metro starts with taking arguably the best metro train in the world to travel to one of the largest shopping malls, to pass through one of the world's largest fountain shows, to get to the entrance of the world's tallest building, Burj Khalifa, to pass back through the mall to see one of the world's largest aquariums inside.

Speaking of which, Dubai certainly is a shopper's paradise, and if you are rich and have a love for shopping, you will likely come Dubai all the time. My first visit allowed me to see the Burj Khalifa. I remember how happy I was since I couldn't believe I had been to the tallest building in the world. Since that was a short trip, it ended with good memories, and I came home with a heavy heart, deciding to save all that I had left for the next time.

One of the cultural shocks that really made me contemplate life and its challenges was the question: "How can the local Emiratis be so rich?" I suppose your first confrontation with any Emirati would be at the airport, stamping your passport, but the second would be when you get out on the road. You will see them driving Range Rovers or probably a Ferrari, making you wonder: is this real life? Who is possibly smart enough to orchestrate a huge invasion of blue-collar workers from countries which are not poor, rather poorly managed, so that those who can't make a good living in their home countries or find themselves in a lesser socioeconomic class can migrate to Dubai with dreams of returning back to their home country with a lot money to start another life with their family?

As a kid, I became used to hearing that a lot of Pakistanis had settled well in Dubai, and someone who forges their trail to get there and acquires a job is very lucky. In short, I grew up believing Dubai was heaven. While I don't disagree that it isn't, with its magnificent architecture it surely is a type of heaven, but after visiting not once but so many times, my perception has changed. I don't want to be very critical, as there are good and bad things about every country, but the bad ones are really bad in my sense, and I have been exposed to them, further strengthening my belief to visit Dubai only as either a traveler or a white-collar employee. It turns out there is no glamour in being the one to build paradise.

What's good about Dubai is, "You can do anything here." Yeah, if you feel like going skiing when the hot temperature warms you enough, you can do the indoor "Ski Dubai" inside the Dubai Mall. Wishing to play golf on a green course in the middle of a desert? Well, you can do that, too. From adventures to food, you can do pretty much everything. Moreover, you can work your whole career working for a big corporation, earning enough to sustain your family, or end up being an entrepreneur, convincing Emiratis to invest in your business. However that ends up, the choice is yours.

My second visit to Dubai came after a year when I traveled for work again and tried to see as much as I left out the first time. From off-road driving in giant SUVs, dune bashing in the Dubai Desert, and visits to beaches, these were highlights of my second trip. Because I went in the winter season, enjoying the desert and beaches was a great idea. The opportunistic chances of becoming a big success are evident from all the separate areas regarding different industries, such as Dubai Internet City for tech companies, Dubai Media City for media outlets, and Dubai Education City for all the schools to be in the perimeter housing for a small colony of educators.

After a while I got accustomed to Dubai traditions and started to remember street names and famous places and made some friends who came with their own benefits. Many of my friends who were recently employed by UAE companies were in Dubai, and I made sure to meet as many as I could in a single trip. Their exhausted and frustrated faces, tired from the day-long work, made me feel blessed to have a proper white-collar job in my country. Probably what attracted them was the tax-free environment, since the UAE doesn't charge income or sales tax, but the scorching heat and tough working environment is what makes you unsatisfied with life. With that, I am not saying every immigrant worker in Dubai is the same. My good friend Faraz, for instance, works for a venture capitalist firm, and he has developed himself as an aspiring entrepreneur that has a good say in the Dubai tech scene, makes a good amount of money, and leads a luxurious life. Dubai's success rates in business imitate a long tradition of an entrepreneurial ecosystem, built up by enthusiastic people who took risks in this new land of opportunities. It is evident that despite the intense Emirate revolution over the past half century, not much has changed in the relationship between growth and opportunity.

As someone who practices entrepreneurship, I have seen many examples of foreign people getting rich by expanding their businesses within Dubai's innovation system; most famous among them being Souk and Careem. Souk, the renowned "Amazon of the Middle East", was finally acquired by Amazon for a hefty 1 billion dollar price tag. A car-hailing ride mobile app, Careem, which has recently made a global name for itself, had been founded by two people not local from UAE but still following in the tradition of creating something out of nothing, the underlying fabric that makes Dubai special. Again, examples such as those make you believe in Dubai. All of these start-ups' rapid growing pace has backing by the UAE's venture capitalists that have empowered these start-ups to grow into full-size companies within a short span of time. If you were to ask me, "What's the thing I like about Dubai?" I honestly am not going to say its buildings or infrastructure; rather, without a doubt, its innovation processes and entrepreneurial ecosystems. Although I haven't been able to launch a company based in Dubai, it has become one of my lifetime wishes to establish a tech company within Dubai. Just like many have followed the American Dream, I want to follow in the footsteps of so many who realize the Dubai Dream.

Honestly, it's the unreformed naff-ness and blustering determination of the city jumping up in just few past decades that I am astonished by. Now with frequent trips to the city and having made many friends, I feel I am on the way to living my Dubai Dream. As early as I can remember, Dubai was an unavoidable pit stop on the way to and from Karachi to the USA.

Now, it has become a city that has captured my heart.

Action Items Related to Chapter Six

1. Research your family ancestors going back two generations until your grandfather. How did it influence you to become what you are right now?

2. List out three things that could be improved about your favorite city. List three things that are actually pretty great about a city you do not like.

Jeffrey Eker Jr. & Sarang Shaikh

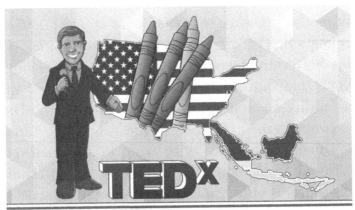

7: THE TEDX STAGE

Lesson: Know when opportunities are life-changing.

So, you have found yourself on the other side of the world getting wired up with a microphone behind a giant stage at a TEDx event. This is the moment you have been dreaming of, something that you have been training for through public speaking engagements your entire life. Watching those TED and TEDx talks in the past, it seemed so easy and fluid, insightful, yet spontaneous.

Rather than watching, this time you are the speaker and have come to learn that those calm voices on the TED stage are actually incredibly rehearsed. Guidelines mandate it, and the immense pressure compels hours of writing and rehearsal. The air behind that stage is thick, a bit hotter than you prefer, and is compressing you, compounded ever more by the honor of speaking on a stage associated with the TEDx organization. Utilizing the energy and enthusiasm paired with the quiet wisp of adrenaline kicking in, you push off that pressure, if only briefly. Your normal eagerness to speak, as you have done dozens of times before, is overshadowed by the absentmindedly pure responsibility of your message being able to live up to the TEDx brand. In April of 2016, as the speaker before me was heard confidently delivering brilliance 20 feet away on the other side of that backdrop, camera angles pierced the air, and stage crew whispered in an unknown language quietly before me, these were the moments before I spoke at TEDx TelkomU in Bandung, Indonesia.

At its core, effective public speaking is about passion. Anyone can learn how to effectively speak before any size crowd so long as they care about and are invested in their topic. The more invested you are, the larger the crowd you can tackle. The larger the crowd you have tackled and become accustomed to, the easier it is to speak powerfully without the support of passion. If you need to speak about something you dread, train yourself by speaking on something you truly care about to become comfortable in front of an audience.

My path to public speaking was not a normal one. It started quite formal and regimented as a Boy Scouts of America Senior Patrol Leader, running our annual Court of Honor or a simple meeting of 50 over-energized little dudes in a church basement on Monday nights. I was not shy about meeting strangers, molded as a front-door-ringing Christmas reef salesman for the annual Boy Scout fundraiser. It grew to engagements like Odyssey of the Mind, where – adorning vast amounts of makeup and a top hat decorated with hundreds of pieces of chewed gum (no, I'm not kidding) – I blasted into the start of our performance dark-faced and ominous, filling the room with, "Come one! Come all! To our creepy carnival!" before proceeding to operate a Rube Goldberg machine. Quirky and fun, after speaking time and time again, my mind developed a completely different mindset when speaking: a switch that could not be flipped unless I was in the moment, in front of people, saying something I thought was important. A strange level of creativity and hyper-awareness, yet inability to focus on anything outside of the task, was at hand. Its own type of uncontrollable high.

As is the case for many important life skills, there was a class for public speaking in college. This one was mandatory, called "Sophomore Clinic II: Public Speaking". Everyone hated it; I absolutely loved it. Slowly building in complexity throughout the semester, the purpose of the class was to ease those not comfortable with public speaking into increasingly challenging public speaking assignments before the class. Through the various clubs and other university opportunities, I had been speaking at multiple engagements, providing a leg up that made this course pretty easy. It was like riding a children's rollercoaster – kind of fun, but a little too simple for any real thrills. Our rather quirky Professor Bingham decided to give the class a challenge, which finally spiced things up. Give the best speech, as voted by the class, for the final assignment and get a 100% on the final exam. It was game on.

The catch? My roommate at the time needed the grade boost and publicly began campaigning for votes. A theater dual major, he was also adept at creative public speaking, and, therefore, a worthy contender who had struggled in some of the previous duller assignments. It was not my proudest moment, but I forged on with secrecy, too thrilled by the idea of chasing down a win. I was blinded to outside sensory input for the week before in preparation, like a lioness focused on an opportunity for prey on the open plains. This was the perfect chance to show my classmates how to chase the vast landscape of opportunities that surrounded them, as I had been doing with my parallel IEEE efforts at the time.

With the sun barely peeking over the horizon and an unseasonable cold in the air, the security guard finally arrived to unlock the building the day of the speech. Despite it being nearly unthinkable in undergraduate times to wake up before 8:00 AM, I had arisen at the crack of dawn to run past the slightly startled security guard into the classroom. Paper taped to the window, window blinds lowered, and Hershey's chocolate deployed below seats, I ran off to my first class in the engineering hall, arriving a bit late – but it was worth it.

The hours passed by.

My enthusiasm rang insatiably through the room as the public speaking class began, the corners of my smile nearly knocking down the cinder block walls of the cramped musty classroom. Walking through how best to chase down opportunity, I reminded my classmates – casually walking over to the windows and pulling the blind strings to raise the shades – that all they had to do was look through windows to chase opportunities. "Sometimes," I said slowly, "you might just find yourself a pot of gold," as I lifted the shade where I had taped a paper pot of gold to the window earlier that morning. Driving the lesson home and securing my final holdout votes, I concluded with reminding everyone that, "In the end you just have to chase opportunities, you never know when you could be sitting on something *sweet* right under you the whole time." Pausing for just long enough for confusion to pierce the air, I smiled, "No, really – I'd check under you now." Sure enough, they found the sweet milk chocolate I had taped under every chair. As they enjoyed their sweet opportunity, I wondered where I had found mine – and what was the foundation of what had grown into such a niche personality.

As far back as elementary school, I remember discussing *Curious George*, an American children's animation, in a one-on-one meeting with our Principal, Mr. Wilson. Unlike most students following the traditional K-12 track, I was lucky enough to have Mr. Wilson follow me and my class along our adolescent journey. From being our principal at Lizzie Haddon Elementary School, to becoming our Haddonfield Memorial High School Principal, he guided us as a passive and powerful mentor. At the end of high school, as he transitioned out of his principal role to join the Haddonfield School Board administration, he paid out of his own pocket to give everyone in my class a small pack of crayons.

He reminded us as he spoke to our graduating high school class at the Tavistock Country Club that all those old people, our parents sitting around us, remembered not the graduating young adult before them, but the small child who would bring back home pictures made with crayons. Never were we to forget their dedication and sacrifice in getting us to where we were that day, a doorway into life beyond their care. As we transitioned into college, living far away from home, we were to remember to use this pack of crayons he was gifting us now to send home a picture every once in a while, to remind them that we cared.

I never had the chance to do so, but I did hang on to those crayons. As my fourth year of college came to a close and graduation loomed, I knew that I was going to draw a picture with those crayons and mail them home to my family. It was only serendipity that brought Mr. Wilson into the engineering hall atrium one sunny afternoon a couple weeks before graduation. Somehow instantly recognizing me, we briefly caught up. He was there to seek a partnership between my old high school and the university, and I was going to use his crayons as the core of our graduating class' commencement speech.

A couple weeks before, I had been honored to be chosen as the student speaker for the College of Engineering at commencement. It was not only a powerful time for us, but also for the university; Henry M. Rowan, the namesake of the university, had passed away several months before. I had been lucky enough to chase him down on his golf cart and get his signature on my "Rowan Engineering" t-shirt that is now proudly displayed next to my diploma, but nobody else would have that opportunity moving forward. It needed to be a speech that paid homage to our mentors, all of them; it had to be a speech centered around those crayons.

Hours after dropping two envelopes in the mail addressed to my home, I pulled that little pack of crayons out of my pocket at the podium in front of all my fellow graduating seniors. This time, it was my responsibility to remind them to be thankful for the loved ones who surrounded them in that packed gymnasium. It is our job to carry on our most important mentors' legacy, from Mom and Dad who got us here, to Henry Rowan who built the university here.

In the end, all public speaking engagements are a privilege, more so now than ever. Never before have we been in an age where attention spans are so low, and just about every person in that room is right on the edge of caring more about their expanding inbox or social media notifications. Nearly all speaking engagements are life-changing opportunities; somehow even those Boy Scout Court of Honors I still remember vividly. I flew out to Indonesia for eleven days right before my last set of university exams to give that TEDx talk because I knew that was an opportunity of a lifetime, and I have never been under so much pressure in my life.

Standing on that stage, crowd before me, projections on either side of me, five camera angles focused in, and the portraits of the Indonesian President and Vice President hung proudly on the wall looking down on me, I completely blacked out. I remember absolutely nothing while giving that speech other than trying to find Qhansa in the crowd who had invited me there to thank her. Never had the switch been flipped into public speaking mode so ferociously that I legitimately needed to wait three weeks to see the video before I confirmed the speech went well, as planned, to a tee. If I wouldn't have mentioned it, nobody would have even noticed the pause where I looked for Qhansa in the crowd.

While I am someone who drives through life insatiably, deriving action items, making lists, executing, and moving forward, this was the first opportunity I can remember that did not feel like a checkbox, but rather a milestone. Everything in my life had prepared me for that moment, to make that accomplishment.

Find those moments in your life; do not simply look for them. When you do happen to find one, positive or negative, reflect, know how you got there – be thankful – and move forward, checking boxes along the way.

Action Items Related to Chapter Seven

1. Turn off your laptop and phone and do not use social media for a day; analyze what you missed during the day and what (if anything) you gained.

2. Ask your best mentor what their most challenging public speaking engagement was and why.

Jeffrey Eker Jr. & Sarang Shaikh

8: DEFINING THE AMERICAN DREAM

Lesson: America is too big for small dreams.

Unintentionally and without resisting, I burped, "Hit the ball!" – not in English, of course, but in Urdu, which I have been speaking throughout my life. On that day in New York City, the mere soberness of a crowd watching a boy missing hits was not understandable to me in any terms, as I carried a legacy of being from a country that has recognition as one of the best in cricket for many decades, and missing a ball was not a success metric to evaluate any player. Failing to resist, I again yelled, "Hit the ball, man!" as I saw sunlight shimmer off the metal surface of the baseball bat as the boy swung it in frustration. I held myself and sighed. What a dejected loser, I thought, as he walked back to the dugout. I smirked, wondering why it would matter to me whether the boy connected his bat with ball or not, although I didn't understand what happened much in the baseball diamond. But there's something about games with bats and balls that never fails to draw my consideration, even at a time like this, when I would soon have one of the most important meetings of my life in New York. I was finally meeting someone, in a manner which my friend Khaled Mokhtar from Egypt would describe as a "Halal Date", since your parents allow and in fact hook you up with each other, for prospects of marriage in the future. However, this particular meeting was only one of many. For now, I will tell you about my first time coming to the US.

My first time was to Boston. I must admit the city has its own significance, and as time has gone on, I haven't been able to resist visiting it again and again. I am not sure whether the presence of top engineering schools such as MIT, Harvard, and Boston State University attracted me to the city or its serenity and welcoming people that took my attention. Just like the shot that was fired centuries ago in Lexington

Square in Massachusetts, exploding the American Revolutionary War, a fire was shot inside my mind, exploding all that it could take when I fell in love with America. The memories haven't faded from the first time I landed at Boston Logan Airport, when they played a Michael Jackson song and I felt, "Woah, I am in America." This was the land of opportunities; this was where I would make my destiny shine.

I came to America for two purposes: a) attend a meeting for an IEEE committee that I was part of and b) showcase my start-up at the Google for Entrepreneurs boot camp. I succeeded in both and experienced some instants that would change my life for the better. Aspiring to become an actor since childhood, all my dreams of Hollywood ascended again, but rather I tried to control my emotions and focus on experiencing much of what America has to offer. I remember once when I was in Philadelphia, I saw this huge quote painted on the side of a building, "America is too big for small dreams," and it kind of resonated with what I believe. I would not come to settle here for something similar or lesser than what I could have achieved in my own country. I don't mean to belittle my country, but we really don't have space for large dreams due to lacking ecosystems, policies, and intellect.

Throughout my life, I always dreamt of belonging to a start-up that had my blood and sweat pouring through its operations to create an entrepreneurial success story this millennium requires, and I knew this was the chance to go big or go home. Well, I went home as nothing much worked that first time; however, I took back the lessons that were good enough to prepare me for globalization and its spirit in my personality.

During my first visit to the US, I was joined by my friend, Subodha, in New Jersey, where we both spent a few days mostly chatting about life and secondly eating Dunkin Donuts until we dozed off. This is where I again reached out to a new contact that I made recently with a cool guy I had met in that Sri Lankan elevator named Jeff Eker, and Subodha and I decided to take a day trip to Philadelphia. We set up a time with Jeff, but little did we know that this would be one of those trips that would take you to understand the value of your life. The warm welcome Jeff gave us – and kept giving us throughout the day – made me realize the purity of globalization. Why else would a native from any country be willing to volunteer to show around travelers from two different cultures? The value was mutually beneficial with the exchange of thoughts and understanding. Jeff took us to two legendary cheesesteak houses that sat staring at each other on opposite ends of the road: the infamous Pat's and Geno's, each claiming to be the king and rightful inheritor of the famous secret recipe of the Philadelphia cheesesteak sandwich throughout history. Jeff was clear about the tiny particular taste differences that both had, but to me, they all taste the same. Of course, this is the same way foreigners treat biryani, the delicious rice dish from Pakistan: they all taste same to them; it is only those of us who have grown up with it that are able to distinguish the tastes. We parted ways, promising to meet and greet each other whenever the chance afforded itself around the world, and I am glad that came true.

America was, in many ways, a life-learning experience for me. One experience that really shook me up, challenging my materialistic goals, was meeting my high school friend. Samee is not only a good-looking guy but an amazing artist. We went to the same high school and he was way ahead of me in many aspects. Among others, these were studies, grades, and hooking up with girls. Being a teenager, I had desired to attain a girlfriend with whom I could have all the romantic conversations, but this goal was never realized due to my low confidence in interacting with girls. I must admit, I was very shy about talking to a girl; however, Samee was a heartthrob of many and had a fan-following ranging from juniors to even seniors. I envied him, but I couldn't do much at that time.

Nonetheless, when I planned to visit Silicon Valley in California, I knew that Samee lived in a town near the Valley and could host me for few days while I looked around. Samee at first hesitated but finally accepted my request to host me at his apartment. I was excited for two reasons. First, surely, I would be visiting all the tech giant corporations' headquarters, including: Google, Facebook, etc., and secondly, a handsome man of character that drew girls in Karachi would be a total playboy living in San Francisco. I knew Samee was the man I was looking for to experience ultimate fun. Turns out Samee was sure the man I was looking for – not for the reasons I anticipated but for those that I never thought would be shared by Samee, and in fact, in San Francisco at all.

He was a changed man now; his life and priorities had changed, and the way he welcomed me in his life for even only three days was enough to make me realize that I had the wrong priorities in life. He had turned religious, become more caring, and overall transformed into a complete man. I was nowhere near his level. For the days that unfolded with his brotherly love and care, I felt huge remorse on my life for motives that came godlike to Samee. I was never a religious man nor an atheist; I was never a good man, nor a bad one. Finally, while I actively prioritized my life, I never chose the right priorities. The Hidayat (as we say in the religion Islam) — the guidance that I was looking for at my home, in my town, and in my country — was never bestowed upon me whilst I despaired and became frustrated from life and its worldly offerings. I was blessed when I saw Samee keeping up his work and being so focused at his life while being surrounded with so much lust and competition. He remained a simple guy with simple goals for his life. Every day he did something to impress me even more.

One day I asked him to take me to a nearby store where I could find Coke. Rather, he made a powdered juice which I didn't resist at first, but when it became a daily routine item, I asked him specifically to get me a soda instead. He gave enough reasons to compel me to at least not consume any soda in front of him as it has its side effects, and besides, we could survive without soda. It was after a while when I came back and understood that change starts small before it turns into transformation. I wanted to change myself, sort of restart my life with new aspirations and goals, so I started to eliminate soda (not completely, but mostly) from my life. The prior level of consumption that touched two regular cans per day soon came down to a regular can once a month. After letting go of my habit of drinking soda, I started to make so many little changes to my life that previously looked challenging and even impossible.

Cultural integration is not one-sided work. A country like the US, which has had a history of its existence and development by contributions of immigrants, sets up a perfect case. For people to understand each other's differences, the spaces between those differences must be given a chance to be appreciated. The new era of the internet and digital media certainly has added much to catalyze the diffusion of globalization. One of the best examples is a website called Couchsurfing, which has been used widely over the past decade by travelers, digital nomads, and people who want to share their couch to get a new friend. When I had the plan to visit California, I didn't know at first the mighty-sized area over which the state is spread. Despite finding my friends, I still wanted a place to stay near Google headquarters in Mountain View to have easy access to its campus and buildings for sightseeing. I was referred by my friend, Ravendar, who also had been hosting friends and been a guest using Couchsurfing in the past, to sign up and make an account to try my luck. I lay awake all night with many cups of coffee to enjoy briefing my whole life to fit inside this Couchsurfing user profile with hopes to find a host that would accept my request for a stay over.

Starting with many rejections, I was finally accepted by a Chinese-American named Yu Wu. Little did I know that this guy would not only be a good host but also a good friend indeed. We exchanged numbers and pictures with each other, followed by setting up a time when Yu volunteered to pick me up from the Mountain View train station. Before I could reach him, Yu was already standing there waiting for me after his work hours. As soon as I disembarked the train, I found Yu and was fascinated by his character. He made all attempts to make me feel at home by sharing his couch, which was smart enough to turn into a queen-size bed, his fridge where I could store my beverages, and his life, into which I had the responsibility to now contribute some value. The thing I like most about Couchsurfing is that it doesn't support any exchange of money/cash between host and guest, rather it encourages you to find each other's sweet spots and values to exchange discussions and cultures to make global friends.

I was Yu's guest for two nights. The first night, I asked him if he knew anybody in Google, since I thought to maybe visit the campus I might have to know somebody to help to let me into the campus for seeing around. Yu answered that I don't need anyone for just visiting the campus. However, the next thing he told me about himself was surely surprising. He shared that he worked for Google and obtained his Ph.D. from Stanford. I was again even more impressed by his accomplishments. We did part ways, but the friendship bond we made was much stronger. We kept in communication, and Yu sent me Christmas cards that year and I promised to bring him some more cultural gifts next time I saw him. We would update each other on our lives and happenings. For example,

Yu joined YouTube and was shifted to downtown San Francisco in an apartment.

Two years after our initial meeting, I was visiting San Jose, California with my professor for a conference presentation, and we wanted a place to stay for two nights somewhere nearby San Francisco to see the Golden Gate Bridge and walk around through all of it. The first time I saw the natural beauty of this bridge was with my friend Samee, who graciously volunteered a Sunday to show me around San Francisco from early morning to late at night. Honestly, these were the people that made my first trip so memorable that I still get chills when I think about them. So now when we wanted to see the Golden Gate Bridge, I knew someone who was a dear friend and would find a way. Although Yu wasn't at his home for the days my professor and I planned to be in his city, he was thoughtful enough to leave his apartment keys in the lock for me to open up and stay as much as I wanted in his apartment. Since I know myself inside out, I will admit I don't deserve such kindness. I am a hopeless loser who has spent many years of life struggling to find his true identity and purpose. There have been so many nights that I can't count to which I would have stayed awake wondering what I have been doing with my life until now. I still believe that it may be a blessing by God, who has provided me with such friends who trust me enough to leave their houses and share their lives with. It is these revelations that satisfy my mind and allow me to sleep at night.

It was once a Friday night in Dallas, Texas where I had a meeting to attend and speak. I had a special next day and had to wake up early, so I needed sleep. But then at that moment, I thought I would go early to the nearest Walmart and look for a cowboy jacket and hat so when my friend Uzair came to pick me up, I would saddle my body with enough cowboy stuff, bandana across my neck, and denim jeans, and speak in the loudest voice as I could to reintroduce myself, "Hey, I think you know me, I am Sarang, the ultimate cowboy!" But then another thought came over me. Why would I do that, when it's Uzair, my buddy whom I was meeting after a gap of 2-3 years now? The lone guy Uzair in the Lone Star State of Texas came all the way over from Houston, his hometown, to Dallas to pick me up – a drive of about 3 ½ hours – and take me back to his home in Houston for a visit. Imagine his excitement to meet me. Uzair and I started to learn and unlearn many things in life. We started playing snooker together and unlearned playing it badly to challenge each to a last-man-standing match whenever we saw each other. Usually, the snooker session for us prevailed for a few hours. We both failed together at many engineering universities' entrance exams, not one or two, but many, and we unlearned it together to earn a bit of success in our lives.

Uzair and I came to Houston to meet cowboys; I mean his family. We spent time remembering the old stories, the girls we had crushes on – and how unsuccessfully we made attempts at making them like us, as well as traveling a lot. There was not a single day when we hadn't left home early in the morning and returned back late at night. After spending a few days in Houston – the small Pakistan version of Texas – we rolled on to the highway, letting the city slip out of sight as we set off into the Lone Star State's highway for exploring other parts of Texas.

The roads extended out as big honking trucks slid past like warriors beside us. Flat grasslands curved into terrific cornfields oscillating in the breeze. A Texas flag dithered above an RV called "American Dreams", and we flung across many scenes to reach the Johnson NASA Space

Center, followed by some highway-based historic places to see. We did try eating Texan steak and burgers filled with juicy chicken smearing the special tasty flavor of Texas. First on our list was Halal Guys, a halal place to eat chicken and meat. The one in Houston had a special item where meat was being smoked over a heated fire, and I asked the guy at the counter to add some more spices into my sandwich. To his surprise, the chef asked, "Where are you from?" and I said "I am from Pakistan." After filling a cup with spicy and tangy onion pickles, he responded, "Here you go, spicy guy." Next up was Taste of Texas, the place for steaks, where we ate smoky and grilled steaks, keeping in mind the restaurant rules: "No barbecue sauce (it doesn't fit well); no forks (look at the end of your arm, they are there); no joking (confirmed by looking at owner's face)." We bid farewell to each other at the Houston Airport after days of enjoyment, where I made my next journey to Los Angeles, California.

I took this excursion to explore the splendor of Los Angeles. While it might be overhyped for Hollywood, beyond the sparkling lights of Hollywood and grit of downtown Los Angeles, the city, which is termed as second-largest in the US, is home to around 75 miles of immaculate coastline covered by more than 35 beaches, many of them loved and cheered by the world in movies and video games. Whether you are a fan of surfing, sunbathing, or simply enjoying cultural traditions, beaches in LA offer almost everything you desire. Now that I have been there multiple times, I have started to remember streets and spots that I personally love and always take people with me to see. I observed that people seem to either love it passionately or hate it all. When I stepped foot for the first time in LA, I was amazed at the ostensibly boundless snarls of freeways that run through the city and the beauties that inhabit its magnificence. I was lucky to find a dormitory right at the onset of Santa Monica beach. I like this dormitory for so many reasons: meeting people from all around the world, sharing rooms with me, making breakfast in hall, and taking tour guide's lessons. For these reasons, over the years I have made it compulsory for myself whenever I am in California to stay, even if for a single day, in that same dormitory. A few of the staff now even recognize me whenever I am there, and they always come up with generous favors since they admire my loyalty to them.

Before I visited, I had images of beaches in LA painting a picture of stationary canals bursting with needles, muscle gyms on beaches tenanted by steroid-pumped Arnold Schwarzenegger look-alikes, and hippies rollerblading along the footpath. Undoubtedly, it encompassed everything in my dreams, but also so much more. Each area of LA has something idiosyncratic to other parts of it: Hollywood with its unabashed fashion, Beverly Hills with its grandiose exhibitions of wealth, and the coastline of beaches filled with unwavering cultural voyages.

Since I have made friends from all over the US, I didn't know that one of my friends who previously was a New Yorker had moved to live in Venice, California. He sent me a message asking where I was staying in LA, and that I should come to stay at his apartment. To my amazement, he was just living on the beach, literally. Adel not only became my host but also my guide, and he told me a few pointers that were quite unique. He said, "If you ever find women squatting seductively or men wandering around in their thong underwear, you shouldn't be surprised." Such is LA.

I must say I am always mesmerized by whatever I see in LA. One of my top favorite moments so far is meeting a Pakistani-

American hotel employee. It was 2016, when I had a three-night stay in a Marriott near Manhattan Beach for a business meeting, that I tried to see most of what I could on my own, since I had a hunch that the recreation department or concierge at the hotel would have expensive options for its guests. I gave it a try anyway on the last day, and I was confronted with this middle-aged bald guy who happened to be Concierge Chief as far as I remember. I read his name, Eli, and I knew instantly it was a nickname for Ali. So I inquired, "What part of world are you originally from, Ali?" He said he was born and raised in Karachi, Pakistan, and in the late '70s moved to the states and had been living here ever since. I happily told him I was from Karachi too, and he was glad to know me, so we sat near to his table and chit-chatted a bit since I knew he was one of my own (you know how comfortable you feel when you see someone from your country and even city). He told me he had never gone back to Pakistan, and he had old memories of Karachi city when it used to be glorious and not very populated. He flooded me with questions, asking about if those places even existed now.

There was one place he said he didn't see since it was constructed in mid-1990s in Karachi, but he had heard from some of his friends that it was the coolest hangout family place to watch a movie and spend time. It was called Drive-In Cinema, a large area with long, widescreen projecting movies. Though there were no chairs and it was not centrally air-conditioned, you would have been seated on your vehicle's dashboards or trunks outside in the open air and environment. I told him, if you ask someone who's born after 1999, they would never tell you that something like that even existed since they demolished the place and made so many shopping and business areas at the start of the new millennium. But as he spoke of it, I was recalling my childhood moments when my father, a smart and powerful man then, took us in his Suzuki four-seater to enjoy the latest movies.

Subsequently, Eli told me his real name was Mehboob, but since Americans had a hard time pronouncing and memorizing it, he opted for Eli as an easy alternative. Because I knew of his age and story, I couldn't call him just by his name; we don't do that in Pakistan for our elders. I couldn't call him Eli if he was in Pakistan; I might have called him Eli Bhai (Brother), Eli Uncle (if he didn't mind) or Eli Sahab (Mr.). I started to call him Eli Bhai, but he insisted I just call him Eli. I said I couldn't do it to his face. Did he think I still would have liked to call him Eli? He smiled and said, "However you wish."

Eli Bhai asked me where I had visited in LA, and I told him I was short on budget, so I had just seen the nearby areas and was saving money for spending on exploring the beaches. He inquired if I had visited Hollywood and the Walk of Fame yet. I said I couldn't afford the cab or even Uber, so maybe next time. He asked me to wait and called one of his friends who came by in his limousine pick me up. I insisted Eli Bhai not do me favors, but he counter-responded, saying, "Do you think I would have left you just like that if it was Pakistan and you were visiting my city and being my guest on my watch?" I thanked him for his generosity. He even offered to take me out for lunch and to stay at his home, but since this was my last day in LA, I promised I would come next time. I must admit, I haven't done well with my promise, and I feel that someday I should surprise him by visiting, but I fear that he won't recognize me. Speaking of his limousine friend, he made sure to take me to every place surrounding Hollywood and Beverly Hills, and I felt like a prince wandering around the most glamorous part of the country, sitting in my suit with a chauffeur in my limousine. Life didn't seem real.

One of the things Eli and I discussed was a story of his kids. Listening to it somewhere in my mind, I recalled a moment from my childhood that was perhaps among the first cultural shocks that I had encountered. As a kid, I didn't have a steady living; my parents both had to move to different cities for work, and so I changed so many schools, which wasted a few years of my life and led me to graduate when I was almost 23.5 years of age, while the usual age of graduation is 21 or at the max 22 for a kid that had straight uninterrupted studies through undergraduate.

There was one city where my father was shifted for some years, and we went there to spend our summer vacations. The place was located near a cantonment colony of officers serving in foreign ministries, military forces, and some oil refineries. There was one family originally from the United States, and the guy was a project engineering supervisor for one refinery to which my father was also assigned duty and had boys of the same age. His father knew my father, and I had a pass to enter the area to play in the grounds. I made friends with Adam, the younger son, who was also a fan of video gaming. Though I used to teach him cricket occasionally, it was playing games on his PlayStation for two hours in the evening that was our most common pastime.

One day, I went up to see him in the afternoon, and his mother, Ma'am Judy, opened up the door, and I asked her, "Can I play with Adam?" She let me through but asked me to wait in the lounge room as they were going to have lunch now. I was so devastated; imagine a teenage boy sitting alone, nothing to do other than waiting for his friend, whose mother was not generous enough to even falsely offer to join them for lunch. I could hear all the chats and sounds of plates and glasses. I left their house crying for reasons I didn't understand in the moment. Maybe it was because I was raised in a culture, more specifically in a Sindhi family, which is more known and admired for its hospitality around Pakistan where a guest meant a responsibility. We would have offered our food (even if the guest came suddenly), our rooms, our time, and in fact a portion of our lives. The most we would do when we didn't want to invite someone to food was to lie that either we were busy or not available, just to not be rude. I could tell when many of my friends' mothers opened

the door and lied that they were taking a bath
or were busy at the moment – even sometimes I
could peek inside and see them eating food – but
that was not as hurtful as the bitter truth that
occurred to me that day when I went to play
with Adam. I was a kid, so I took it to my heart
and thought maybe I was the bad one there. It
was when my father shared with me that this is
how most of the people in the West live, that I
was made to understand this is not their fault
and this is not ours, it's just a different culture,
and each has its own values and significance.

Over the years when I interacted with people
from Western countries and met them
personally, I observed there's a lot of
"individualism" among them, which makes them
stay alone and be self-interested, not knowing
what friendly hospitality looks like. However,
countries like mine (Pakistan, India, etc.) have a
lot of family built-in systems, and so not only
our immediate but even extended families stay
in touch. We have a culture of too much sharing
in our lives, even if we have fewer of these
interactions. I found some friends were shocked
when I brought them gifts; they asked me
repeatedly, "Why did you buy me a gift?"
although they did admire the point. To be
honest, there was no real point; it's pretty much

common for us to bring gifts, although I will admit sometimes we enjoy it during family gatherings. One time, I was to meet a professor at a café in the US state of Rhode Island, and I brought him a Sindhi culture ajrak (a beautiful traditional cloth) as a gift. He thanked me and gave me his umbrella on the spot, saying he had one extra in his bag, since I didn't know that it would rain that day. I thanked him, but he said, "No, thank you. You gave me ajrak, I gave you an umbrella. We are equal now."

Once at Boston, Massachusetts, I happened to meet an old lady while waiting for my train. I chatted for a while and offered her my snacks. She was happy and asked if she could sit with me for the rest of journey. I said yes for sure, and she opened up her purse and tried to give me a 20 US dollar bill, smilingly saying, "Thank you for your time and snacks today. I realized I ate one whole packet of your chips so this is the amount for that." I was embarrassed and didn't take her money. I mean, I didn't sit with her so she could tip me! This was also one moment which for me was very natural. In Pakistan we would have done it without even asking, and the beneficiary of our deed would have assumed by default for us to step up and help.

Another time I was traveling from LA to San Jose, California. Here was this pretty old lady who had luggage stacked up in front of her. Someone I am assuming was her son had dropped her in front of me, and after questioning from some local, he had stacked up all the luggage at a spot where the tourist bus was to arrive and left. Unfortunately, the bus parked at a distance and before she even could ask anyone for help, I stepped forward, motioning her to get inside the bus and I would load the luggage in the bus. I did it because she was pretty old, and there was no way she could have lifted all that up on her own. I did it without any reward to be compensated. She thanked me the whole way, and when the bus took a stopover for lunch, she insisted, or should I say begged, to allow her to pay for my lunch.

For me all these efforts, gifts, and initiatives mean nothing special; I can go either way as its set up by default in my personality. I am not saying they offend me, but they are shocking to me as I am used to getting my hands into everyone's lives, helping them and making the most of it.

Yet, having said all this, I also saw the other side of personalities in the US, especially those living with a much more culturally-oriented mindset. Their personalities were defined by more openness; they were more welcoming and community-oriented. It was indeed people like Jeff, who opened his arms to always make me feel comfortable. I knew that I would have a place to stay and a friend to talk to whenever I was in Philadelphia, and that I wouldn't necessarily have to return his favors. It was people like Ussash Arafat, a Bangladeshi who had settled in America, who came over to meet me with his wife when I was in Los Angeles. It was Karen Bartleson, the IEEE-mom, as I say, who was always eager to see and meet me. I never felt any difficulty in approaching her; she was a lady that could make you feel special. It was people like Yu Wu, who opened up his house for me to stay and live even when he was not around since he believed in exchanging cultural thoughts.

I could go on and keep mentioning an entire list of people, but I believe I have made my point that there are two sides for sure – the second of which I had never expected to see in Americans. That's the answer I always give when people of the stereotypical mindset ask me, "Why do you love to go to states when it's so racist and selfish?" I respond that there would be a very minimal percentage that might be racist or selfish and most people I met are those that admire you and your belongings. In fact, this is the same answer I give to even those Westerners that ask, "How do you live in Pakistan when it's terroristic and bad?" The answer is the same; there will be a very tiny percentage of people that might have bad intentions, otherwise, all don't think the way the media portrays.

Speaking of America being an opportunity land, I once had a chance, or I must say privilege, to travel on a budget airline. Though I have traveled on one in Europe, this one was way on the budget-side for sure. With budget restrictions and aspirations for adventure, my creative mind made me look out for alternatives such as this. Inundated with so many selections for the route, I found a budget airline – one that offered a ticket for only $1, that's right, just one buck – for a distance from DC to Boston. This also is an effect of globalization, that today's flying experiences have become much like traveling in a cheap bus, not the unreal golden era of the 1950s of gentlemen and ladies, men fully suited, and women with white gloves and fancy hats. This is where the budget airlines have created a whole new market and have made it easy for anyone to travel. But it comes with a compromise of so many things that we might have taken granted or at least that I have had throughout my life. Confined planes, substandard customer service, hidden fees, and no frills in flight. In the end though, these budget airlines are useful when you are way too restricted in your budget.

It's quite a dilemma to decide whether to travel by a budget airline or not, since you know you will have limited options when you are on a $1 ticket. You know there will be no reclining seats, no free food, no free checked bags, let alone free entertainment onboard. I could live with all these compromises, but what shook me and literally staggered my mental condition was when the budget airline started charging you for using the restroom.

My travel experience on a budget airline was no more than a horror story. I was embarrassed throughout the flight for various reasons. Firstly, I never knew the budget airlines in the US, perhaps being modest in their infrastructure, would not have a separate counter to check in. So I spent a lot time wondering where to submit my luggage. I saw some people that looked to me like homeless or maybe hopeless, with their torn attire and sickened personality, carrying the same airline boarding pass. Following them, I got to know that it's fine to rent out counters in the US for checking in your passengers for a flight. But again, who was I to complain about a $1 flight ticket? Upon reaching my seat, I got to know there's literally nothing that I could do onboard. The seats were just like normal seats, but the worst was yet to come when I unintentionally went to the restroom to take a leak and came out to see an air hostess – a young, gorgeous, and sensual lady – staring at me to ask me something important. I exchanged a quick smile and expressed to myself, "Wow, what a beauty," and as I stepped forward, she broke the silence and enquired, "How would you like to pay for that, sir?" I was taken aback; I didn't recall what I did that I had to pay for. I mean, I hadn't taken a bath, I know that calls for a payment; I hadn't ordered any snacks, since I had traveled on some other budget airlines and knew that they charge you for food; so, it was unclear what she was asking for.

I inhaled a deep breath, and my mind had thoughts. Did she know that I was looking at her like some creep? Maybe her asking for money can be a taunting way to mock me for my behavior. What do I respond back with? Should I stay firm and confidently say, "You are mistaken, perhaps, I was never looking at you," or perhaps I should confess and apologize for my behavior, as deep down I did feel guilt from being that creep, but again, that was so involuntary. Having these options in mind, I asked her, "Ma'am, pay you for what... looking at you?" She half nervous and half red-faced responded, "No, you just used the restroom. That's $5 for the first five minutes." What? This wasn't real. What airline charges you for using the restroom? But I pondered on the thought, who am I, complaining on a $1 ticket?

In my opinion, I have trust that without trips to Alaska or Hawaii, you haven't really seen the whole US, as many say when they road trip from the Pacific to Atlantic coasts. From the icy glaciers of Alaska to the volcanic sands and beautiful beaches of Hawaii, if you haven't seen any of it, I pity you.

I had the chance to say "Aloha" once in my life. I had a once in a lifetime visit to Hawaii to participate in a strategic session with the IEEE Board of Directors and leaders. They decided the location for the event would be on the Hawaiian island of Oahu at the Four Seasons hotel at Ko Olina. I was among the twelve invited young professionals from around the world by IEEE President Karen Bartleson, to contribute my learnings and experiences. I will try to put down the experience of Hawaii in words, but I am definite I can't justify the feelings that I had and moments that I experienced accurately.

It was magical for me, no less than a dream. Try to picture this scenario and honestly ask if I really deserved to be there. I was invited to travel in business class for my contributions to help my community, country, and the global organization. It was an honor to be among those twelve that were the chosen ones. I landed in the Honolulu Airport with a small carry-on bag and a tired body since it was not one, two, but three flights that were required to make the journey. In total, the whole journey was 20 hours in flight and 10 more hours including layovers and taxiing. I was exhausted when I landed in Honolulu. There was a guy from the hotel waiting to pick me up. He came all dressed up to welcome me in his Cadillac, a brand which I never had the opportunity to ride in before. The resort where all of us stayed was a bit far from Honolulu on the island Oahu. When I reached my room, unpacked my luggage, and changed into my night clothes, I contemplated on mere feelings. I was finally in Hawaii. This is was; this was where I always dreamt to come, and now I was here as a delegate. A sense of responsibility prevailed over me, and I decided I would not be a dummy; rather I would contribute as much as I could, since so few from my city, my country, and in fact in IEEE globally, get this chance. So if I have earned it, I better be justifying the opportunity.

The President, who was gracious to invite me, believed in my potential. I reflected on 2015, when I was in the Silicon Valley area and she was still working with a company, about to retire, and I traveled from one city to another to meet her. Since she had been a great supporter and Facebook friend, and there was no chance at that time for her to be IEEE President in the future, my intention was not of greed (as a lot of people conspired after they saw me talking there). I believe in investing in people; to me, financial investment comes after investing in human capital. If I see someone I can get learning from, or is sweet and caring in nature, I will go to all lengths to meet, greet, and in fact assist them, not because I want something in return from them but because I want to contribute to the betterment of this world. The least I can do is give my time and thoughts. That meeting with Karen was followed by a lot of discussions, comments, and talks over the years. Finally when she became President, she was already aware of my potential, and I had a working relationship with her for a few years which brought me to where I was now, at that very moment, totally awake at night, not able to sleep due to excitement in Hawaii.

Situated on the coastline of Oahu's rocky Western coast community, the hotel preserved a very beautiful view of the beach and the ambiances it housed. I, along with my other young professional friends, had decided to find time to visit the famous Waikiki Beach, but it was far away from where we were staying, so we would have to rent out a car. Luckily, I met someone who introduced himself as Vice President for one of the boards of IEEE, Samir El-Ghazaly.

As usual, I never had an idea that this man would end up being one of my mentors from whom I would seek career guidance. He offered some of us the opportunity to join him for dinner in Honolulu downtown one evening. Though we had our own plans, he was so sweet that we couldn't resist and joined him for a session. He already had a car and he took us to an amazing seafood place where we ate wholeheartedly and took a small stroll around the downtown and its streets. Meeting people like Samir and staying in contact afterwards is one of those life-changing moments for me. He has never said no to any of my requests, including an invitation to a conference at Pakistan in April of 2018, where I had the pleasure to host him and take him around for a small city tour of Karachi.

Staying in Hawaii, we decided to move around like Hawaiians, and that's by wearing Hawaiian shirts. We purchased a couple and attended our meetings wearing those shirts. It was later that one of my dearest friends, Kathleen, who is based in California, decided to print customized Hawaiian shirts for all of the IEEE members in this Western region of the United States, and she was kind enough to gift me one. On the last day, I stayed a day more and personally went to see Waikiki Beach and its beautiful scenery. Having watched the hula dance, I purchased a showpiece magnet of a girl wearing a Hawaiian dress that performed hula dancing whenever sunlight graced its micro solar panel. With many promises, lifetime memories, and souvenirs, we all departed Hawaii. It was dreamlike.

The good thing about the US is its huge size and the diversity of cultures it brings. Honestly, this did translate into some bad side effects. For instance, the big-sized offer of ... everything. You buy a pack of chips, they don't come small; you buy a small coffee and the smallest they have is enough to caffeinate me for a year; you try to get a small tour of the country, not possible with its sheer size.

Visiting the US and not spending days in Washington, DC or on the streets of the widely known New York, Brooklyn, and Queens means you haven't seen everything the US has to offer. Apart from being the capital of all the states, Washington, DC is a classy family destination. Folks often like to come with their kids to show them the history of their people, the country, and nation itself. Wandering around DC won't be the same as cities in other states, since the city will give you a chance to see where the US President lives, where the dollar bills are made, where the tombs of the freedom fighters rest, and a multitude of museums to understand US history. Being a budget traveler, I first came to DC to spend a few days to experience the history of this country and to have meetings at an IEEE office there. I got a recommendation to stay at a dormitory called HI Hostels, which has a huge chain of hostels all around the US. I took the membership on the spot, considering it to be my crashing place in each city wherever I would go in the US. Apart from cheap living, the hostel has indoor games installed such as snooker, board games, and a social space.

I am an average player at almost every board game and play snooker well. In high school, I was a big fan of outdoor games such as football, cricket, and tennis, but these boring board or table games which can be played inside a room or a hall never really came into my field of interest. I couldn't fathom the importance of learning them back when I was a kid. Nevertheless, when we (me and my friend Uzair) went to join a coaching academy after high school to prepare for the entrance exams of engineering schools, things changed. Luck had it all, since the building where the coaching academy was situated had a snooker club on the top floor, and one of our friends convinced us to learn this game. Initially we played to pass time, but gradually our tutor friend made us understand its importance. He said he had played the game to impress so many people, and that it also helps to break the ice when you are meeting strangers, assisting you to speak with them in a language that might not be in words but through this game.

That was nearly a decade ago, and I thought: that's a good motivation to learn, but I am not getting out of this country, so where would I use all that for building up connections? It was DC. Of course, the hostel had a giant snooker table, and I saw a couple of people from different nations staying at the same hostel, playing each night after they were all exhausted and tired from their daily strolls of the city. So one evening, I greeted them and asked if I could play. There was a group of two girls from Poland, a group of teenage boys from Africa, and some Mexicans who were not good with speaking English. Surprisingly, I beat them all one by one.

The manager asked the next morning if I was the guy who defeated everyone last night. I said, "Yeah," and he asked me to wait. I thought maybe it's illegal to beat everyone in snooker when you are Pakistani – haha, the old stereotypes that sit toxic in your mind – but this guy came back with his stick and asked if we can do a best-of-three match series right now. Of course, if someone comes with their stick and it's their place, chances are strong you will be defeated, and I was indeed defeated that morning. But the game itself helped me make so many friends. A night earlier, I was a stranger drinking soda and watching movies sitting in a lobby; while tonight, I was the famous brown guy that plays snooker like hell. With my new friends, we went together to see the typical sites in DC such as the White House, Washington Monument, the Capitol, and the Lincoln Memorial.

It's good to see such things; they make you appreciate the connotation of breathing in a democratic society. However, studying in Pakistan, I always, like millions of others, studied history simply to pass. In fact, the only subject that we studied repeatedly throughout school until engineering school was Pakistan Studies, and even that was taught in a very boring style, leading almost none of us to really get the essence of our history. Thus, a sense of guilt came to me when I stepped foot into many museums and saw the dedication of staff and the US government for how they preserved each piece to make their citizens value the dignity, peace, and lives they live. I felt the worth of being an American citizen. It's unfortunate to have such a rich culture and museums in Pakistan with all of them very poorly managed and the administrators never imparting a sense of citizenship within us.

In those three days in DC, I visited as many museums as I could. We had a group of friends that had every category of person. Soon, on the wishes of science lovers, we went to see the Smithsonian National Air and Space Museum to see how technology has advanced throughout eons. The boys from Africa in our group wanted to see the National Museum of African Art to distinguish their cultural values that have been brought to the United States. But as I was told from my friends, you can't see the whole DC in a few days; rather you need weeks and months to see everything. That's when I promised my new friends and the city of DC to return back, and I have returned back – two times after my first trip. I like this city so much – it is always full of surprises.

It was also remarkable to see the White House, AKA the place where decisions are made to run the US, and I saw many people protesting outside of its barriers. For my friends from Europe and other areas, it was an entirely new or not-so-common thing, and they asked us to either wait or go and they will join us. For me and one of our Indian friends, sadly or luckily, we belong to countries where we have people protesting for food, water, electricity... to almost everything practically every day, so I am used to watching and, in fact, participating in these protests.

Whereas Washington might shock you with its rich, historic scenes, New York, on the other hand, takes exactly a minute to spoil your eat, travel, and experience caprices. You will see a lot of crowds and a lot of noise, and if you love being surrounded by so many people, you might love it, but I didn't. It's like you come here, see around some famous hyped-up places, and now stagger through a gorgeously volatile city that invites you to find someone who's against your expectations or vice versa. The city of New York might be famous for its streets and all, but I say it's more than a city, it's a hub of cultures. You'll see people doing things you have never seen. People into stuff that would be taboo as per your culture but is very well defined and accepted for them, and you'll find almost everything that you wish for in terms of food, traveling, and experiences. With its vibes and the humans of New York themselves, you have to be extra loud, flirty, and alert to experience the city in its true sense. To me, the city perfectly describes the saying, "Go big or go home." I say there are chances even to go much bigger than big, so nothing but self-doubt and naysayers will conspire to stop you.

Visiting New York for the first time, what I found common between it and my city Karachi was that as a visitor, you must be your own person. The active city people are rat-racing through their daily chores and schedules, the natives are too busy with their lives, the poor are running cycles of either begging at you or cheating you on the streets, while you, the visitor, get to experience the city that has people rushing through winds in order to make up their lives and earn enough to afford an exorbitant rent and basic life.

As it was my first trip to New York, I wanted to find some New York special foods, and I tried asking the busy-running natives, and almost everyone was stuck at, "Uhhh... you see... uhh..." Perhaps their minds were too overcrowded with thoughts on paying rent and affording their car, or they were too confused to suggest something. So on my next trip after a year, I got some hints from my New Yorker friends that its better you ask them, "Where do you eat when you are in a good mood?" and they'll throw out so many options. What I like most about New York, in fact most of America but specifically New York, is whenever you want free Wi-Fi or want to take a piss, you'll find a well-maintained publicly accessible internet hotspot and public restrooms: I like to call them "Starbucks".

But that's not the only thing that brings me to Starbucks. What I actually do whenever I am back in the States and Starbucks is nearby – which it always is of course – is order my favorite large latte coffee. I was a huge fan of cappuccino, but Starbucks made me fall in love with latte.

I am not a big fan of parks, but a lot people suggested I go to Central Park in New York City. I always thought it must be the same as every park, until one day I meandered through Central Park and was taken aback with its vastness and nature. One end of it will even jump you directly to Times Square, yet it is so large that whatever plans you make, you'll be late and tired. So I always try to stick to a few places and enjoy them rather than running around multiple places in minimal time.

Although I have been more than five times to New York, due to the vastness of Central Park and pretty much everything in the city, I still feel there's a lot left to see. Some things are quite common about New York that perhaps someone who has lived almost all their life in Karachi would understand. Sidewalks in New York (this is what they like to call it, however we simply call it a footpath) are sort of like highways. You can't stop in the middle of walking, not intentionally or even mistakenly. Just like on a highway, you have to take sides, otherwise busy-going people will either ram into you or you'll fall down by getting shoved from walkers. You know you can't walk just for taking a walk; you should walk with purpose. It applies the same on roads, both in Karachi and New York, that people will honk horns at you if you stop or even slow down on a road. Don't attempt to slow everyone else, and this is the most that you can do for the citizens. What's more common? Getting to see side-way eateries and rickshaw-style food trucks, mostly pedaling on bicycles. The food is cheap and fast for people who are not necessarily cheap but fast for sure.

Despite all that, I will not say I like New York. I do, however, like Jackson Street, where I visit every time I am there. The significance of this street is its cultural embrace of local Pakistani culture: people selling desi foods and sweets in desi unhygienic style, beggars on the roads troubling you, and a lot of really spicy food. Jackson Street goes by "Little Pakistan". I like watching how cultural values change the whole scenario. You get out of Jackson Street, and you feel you are back to the land of dreams, but once you are there, you'll automatically feel you're in Pakistan.

There's still a lot that I can speak about for New York, but I will take a break because I think this one chapter will not be enough to suffice its nature. However, everyone's usually happy wherever they are in the world, as long as they feel safe. Although I am proud and happy being in Pakistan, I do carry an "American Dream". My dream is pretty much in pursuit to be fulfilled; the largest evidence is this book itself that I share with this amazing friend, Jeff, who's more than a friend, colleague, and coauthor — an embodiment of my vision and ambition, despite our inhabiting opposite sides of the globe.

Before I end this chapter, I know you guys and gals would be wondering: have I been to Las Vegas yet? Well, I did it twice. In my earlier trips traveling to the US, it was among the to-visit places for sure. I didn't know what I would I do alone, but the excitement got the most of me, and I booked a room using Airbnb just a little way from the Strip and arrived taking a chartered bus service from Los Angeles. I must say, Las Vegas, at its very first impression, disappointed me fully. Every time you see it in movies and media, they show you this ostentatiously enhanced Vegas and its unusual lifestyle, but little are you informed about what lies beyond these lights and flashes. Taking the perception that once I would put my feet on Vegas, I thought I would be surrounded by casinos and strippers. In reality, the bus stop dropped me far away from the city, and it was just a damn hot day in October.

I called an Uber and a middle-aged lady who happened to be of an Iranian origin took me to my place. She told me two things that I couldn't have guessed at first glance: first, the Las Vegas airport had not been international for so many years, and second, it's just that Strip – a long road for many miles – where you have these acclaimed Vegas spots. Otherwise, it's just a normal boring city that doesn't pay well.

My utter frustration to have a lady pick me up in full clothing grew worse when I arrived at my staying place, and it was so far away from the Strip that I would in no proper means be able to walk there. Integrity was dismissed by my host for sure when she mentioned that her house was only 20 minutes walking away from the Strip, though in truth, I once huffed it to the Strip, and it took me around 55 minutes to walk. The same Uber lady warned me the people of Vegas, especially in the Strip, are frauds. The house had a swimming pool in the back, which calmed me enough to not complain to Airbnb or the host, and so I changed my attire and jumped into the pool to cool myself.

I was joined by a big-sized guy, wearing violent tattoos all over his body and smoking a cigar in the pool. We exchanged greetings, but I was afraid of him since he had a fearful aura that pissed me off. When he closed near and started conversation, however, I found him sweet. He was also an engineer who came here to interview for an IT support job in one of the top hotels. I asked him how I can better reach the Strip without taking any taxi, and he said, "With me, in my car." So he gave me an offer to join him at night, and while he was busy looking up his place, I could roam around, and once I got tired I could call him up and he would be there to pick me up. This way I made a new friend who not only chauffeured me but also gave me tips about how to find the best drinks, prostitutes, and gambling. To his absolute shock and disbelief, I told him I happen to be a straight guy not into drinks, sex, and gambling, making him ask me, "Why are you in Vegas, then?" I said, "To feel a hangover."

Before visiting Vegas, I watched the movie *The Hangover* and really liked how the four friends had a respite from their normal life by getting a hangover in Vegas. I did wish to have three friends accompanying me so we could have our version of the hangover, but instead, I was there to watch around. You ask me how Vegas is? It's a land of desert that has significantly renovated into one of the most lavish places of earth. The Strip makes it an appealing place to party, but beyond it, the natural beauty and local gifts can also impress you, if you seek them out. Vegas, as claimed, is all about living life to the fullest. It's a huge expanse of a thing that's alive with a pulse of disordered energy that you'll find amazing.

In my first tour, I walked through the whole Strip and sat on a rollercoaster for the second time in my life, and also for the first time alone as a traveler. It was scary, yet in parallel enthralling. At night, I would walk around bars and clubs to see strippers pole dancing and seducing, and then transition to sip shisha (hookah) around the corner at one of the cheapest bars in the town. It was in Vegas when I first tried the juicy steak burger of the famous Master Chef Judge, Gordon Ramsey. It was expensive – but totally worth it. That was the kind of hangover that I wanted from this trip. I enjoyed my time, bought some souvenirs, and planned to come over with some friends next time. I didn't know it would come very soon after when, in 2017, I, along with three other friends, made a plan to rent out a car to travel to Vegas from Arizona (where we were all gathered for a meeting). We began sprinting down highways to the land of nightlife.

When you are nearing Vegas, the city is situated in a sort of valley, and it's almost like you're driving inside of a bowl with city lights flashing beneath like you are in a board game, encircled with these misty blue desert elevations. So the four of us took a trip just like in the movie *The Hangover* to have our own kind of hangover. This time, my mind was blown right away since our friend – our chauffeur for the whole trip and guide (so we gave him the title "Supreme Leader"), Khaled Mokhtar, booked us to stay in the pyramid-shaped hotel called Luxor at the

Strip. I couldn't believe I was staying on the Strip, and in fact, in such an extravagant hotel.

Taking a night to rest, we went beyond the Strip to a shopping area that had grassy parks and benches to rest. It was amazing to see this side of Las Vegas where people are normal; they enjoyed natural beauty and they were not showy. But as you stepped inside the Strip, casinos were everywhere you looked, in fact not just casinos but gas stations, restaurants, and gambling – everywhere. It was funny to me whenever I saw maniacs super drunk carrying their zombified bodies to press slot machine plungers to try their luck, to perhaps double their bet money. The alleyways were littered with little photo cards of naked or in-bikini women, and upon closer examination you would see they were business cards for call girls and prostitutes. What's strange is that there are people hired to distribute those to everyone walking around.

Another strange thing that I always find in Vegas is the lunatic behavior of some people. Once I was walking around the Strip, and suddenly a few boys came screaming and running towards me with their arms raised over their heads. When they came near, they exclaimed, "High five buddy, high five!" and so I did, and they danced and high-fived each other as if it was a task for a scavenger hunt that they had filled. Once a lady approached me to take her picture and I did. She came over, saw it, and said, "No, it looks too boring. Can you take it again?" I said sure, and she literally started to take off her shirt and pants so I abruptly stopped her saying, "I can't take your picture like this!" I was afraid because this could have been a trap to lure me into sexual activity or something like that, but I stood there and saw that more than a threat to anyone, she was mentally ill and doing it purposefully to show around her assets to everyone for nothing.

At last, they say, "Whatever happens in Vegas stays in Vegas." So I will stop sharing some of our experiences. Nevertheless for me, the American experience, journey, and dream have yet to be finished. I have a lot to see still and a lot to experience. My personal goal is to visit all 50 states by 2019, and I have plans to achieve it. I have plans also to pursue my American Dream, which I already have started, although it doesn't look like what people typically assume it to be: getting settled in the US, becoming rich, and living life to the fullest. I have my own beliefs for the American Dream, which are inspired by today's effects of globalization.

For me, the American Dream is not about pursuing monetary opportunities, but instead experiencing how to develop the means to both see and seize it. If the internet has caused globalization, it has also made real opportunities to encompass you in the boundaries of trust, wisdom, and sharing. It's in your hands to make it vulnerable and abuse it for your greed or utilize it to earn the opportunity to produce that lifetime experience, which is certainly more than just making money.

Uber provides you with a fleet taxi service at your doorstep and makes sure you make the most out of your journey. On most of my Uber rides I have opted to sit in the front with driver and chat about their life. They often surprisingly opened up to me and delivered more than just service as an Uber driver, building from a customer relationship to being more like friends. I have earned the opportunity to live free in houses of people like Yu Wu and some others via the Couchsurfing service. This is what makes it beautiful. In the past, opportunities to become global were available for those who would find it on their own, but today you must be able to successfully traverse yourself through technology and filtering options to get the most within your comfort zone. Out of the box, today, it's about how your internal filter assesses effectively to manage knowledge and wisdom equally. The American Dream of the past stimulated hope and brightness, as everything was possible for anyone via their own means, and thus, people immigrated to live a better life. But today with this web of the virtual world, almost everything is possible by sitting in your home. Having earned the right to grasp those opportunities now unveils a responsibility, requiring a set of abilities that must be learned to filter through the noise and avoid missing your chance to seize the opportunities that are right for you, wherever they are in the world.

Action Items Related to Chapter Eight

1. Travel to a city you have never been to and spend the weekend in a hostel.

2. Create and actively manage a list of your favorite city for: Nightlife, Culture, Working and History.

Compare your list with those you meet around the world.

9: LAUNCHING CULTURECLOUD AT THE RIO OLYMPICS

Lesson: Entrepreneurship is about focus – time is your biggest enemy.

When Angie said the word, "Miracle", back in high school, I ended the traditional back and forth of converging on a career ambition. My answer for the longest time had always been, "Sculptor at LEGO Land", when asked what I wanted to be when I grew up. For some kids in kindergarten, it might be teacher, fireman, or policeman, evolving as we aged. As we grow older, especially in the digital age, we find that the question is no longer, "What do you want to be when you grow up?" rather, "What will drive your career ambition when you grow up? Where do you see yourself in 5 years?" After all, what sort of definition can you attach to a "digital nomad", anyway?

I had my career ambition dead set on making an impact in spreading the power of international perspective. Thus far, I had the opportunity to study abroad in Germany, helping myself spread the power of international perspective. I had then leveraged that experience to create the Australian-American IEEE student branch exchange with my friend in Australia. With that, I had the opportunity to spread international perspective to over 100 students digitally and physically bring 10 students to Australia. Great!

But lying on a conference room table at about 1:00 AM in the Honors Wing of Whitney Hall at Rowan University during the spring of 2015, a couple of my best engineering friends and I brainstormed. How could we create something that spread the power of international perspective to everyone; what would be the best way to start? While we wouldn't rationalize our thoughts from that late-night daze for some time, the answer came from one phrase: most of the time when you travel, the best adventures aren't about where you are, but who you're with.

What if you could literally place yourself on the map and instantly filter to find both travelers and locals who shared your similar interests? Why not engage local ambassadors to feature culture-defining businesses that you wouldn't normally find as a tourist on that same map too? I remember sitting up on that conference room table and thinking... "Holy shit, we have to make this." The issue was – the only thing we knew was how to make it. And how to name it: CultureCloud®.

Literally, we knew how to make it – we were a room full of engineers. To us, the "making it" part was easy enough. While no part of software development is easy, the secret most engineers don't want to tell you is: it's all about what you remember having googled how to do in the past and properly typing your new questions into the search engine when you're drawing a blank. In the end, most everything can be found in forums. That night, I sat in that conference room excited that I was going to learn how to code in Android; to this day, however, I have not coded a single line of CultureCloud.

My internship that summer had brought me up to the Boston, Massachusetts area where I spent most of my day driving out to clients, analyzing manufacturing automation at factories, identifying gaps in systems, designing solutions for those gaps, and then communicating them to everyone, from the guy on the floor to the CEO, in the hopes of selling automation equipment. My friend, fellow engineering student, IEEE volunteer, and roommate Charlie had gotten me the position; we were juggernauts of the role. Initially brought together designing a robotics competition, we had built an incredible infamy, relentlessly raising money through industry sponsorships for our IEEE initiatives at Rowan. We were so effective that the university was afraid we would disrupt some of their large-amount pursuits. They admonished us for our success, and stood up a whole new process in case students were ever as successful at fundraising in the future.

We were both incredibly motivated and energetic, thriving off the opportunity for a challenge. For that reason, Charlie had come up to Boston for us both to complete a joint project for the intern innovation challenge (which we were happy to eventually win), and to launch our first CultureCloud beta version of the mobile app.

Shortly after our late-night conference room think tank session a couple months back, we had assembled a development team of Brad, Samed, Charlie, Austin, and me. Brad was the web guy, Samed was the Android guy, Austin was the iOS guy, and Charlie and I were the business guys. Or at least so we labelled ourselves. In truth, we needed to learn everything we needed to accomplish on a whim, when the need presented itself. Engineers paddling through uncharted waters, we had ascertained that we needed non-disclosure agreements and knew enough to reach out to some lawyers to see whether we could patent the software and exactly how to go about setting up our legal business infrastructure.

By July, our months of work had paid off. Charlie and I were working out the last kinks with Samed on the phone as we sped in an Uber toward Cambridge, Massachusetts for the 4th of July celebration and fireworks, where we would approach as many people as possible to get our beta community started. As Charlie and I plowed down the "Mass Pike" highway toward the heart of Boston in our Uber, we worked to wrap up the final coding glitches in the CultureCloud messaging feature over the phone with Samed ahead of our big unofficial kickoff.

Anyone who has been in a start-up before knows exactly where this was going. Nowhere. In fact, we didn't even make it to the starting line; about 40 minutes into the Uber ride, it became a sobering clear reality that the mobile app beta was completely broken, and even if we did fix the glitch, it would take hours for Google to process it onto the store and for Apple (at the time), days to do the same. Moreover, we carried no type of advertising material, targeted no specific event location, and both our phone batteries were running low from the nonstop testing. Diagnosis? We were engineers, not business people.

People-watching in Cambridge is an especially interesting experience. You are surrounded by the typical Boston "MassHole", extremely intelligent MIT students, and clueless tourists such as us. We drank some abysmal-tasting tequila, wandered through the halls of an MIT building, and eventually found an unlocked door to climb up onto a pyramid on the roof of MIT's Great Dome building above the Department of Civil Engineering. Sitting alongside 20 or so other illicit unlocked-door-finders, we gazed down on the crowd, enjoyed an ambitious fireworks display, and allowed the reality to set in: we were going to have to roll up our sleeves and work hard, really hard, to make CultureCloud happen.

As the last few weeks of the summer rolled around, I moved into my friend's closet and continued working every day after returning from a day's work at my internship. I would be in the kitchen on my laptop when she left and would often remain in the same spot hogging the small kitchen table in her apartment above a garage until late in the evening. The CultureCloud team knew that we had to get smart, and more and more it became obvious that my role would be to never touch the software of this business if it were to succeed; rather, I had to learn to do business.

Hours and hours were spent pouring through legal template websites and attempting to graduate from the janky non-disclosure agreements we had printed out after clicking the first link Google had returned a couple months back. Knowing that we had to find ways to integrate the business into our coursework to free up time, we began an application to start an Engineering Clinic project for CultureCloud. This is similar to a Senior Design Project at most universities. After getting approved, it allowed us to bring a sizable team onto the project. Students would get course credit, and we would make progress – all the while using that new business acumen to have those students and the college agree that we would maintain all intellectual property in contracts. Finally, in September that year, we signed the papers to officially form Tediferous, LLC, a name which, credit where credit's due, my friend Josh had contrived the summer before while we were at our summer internship trying to find cool names to call our business if we ever started one. He won that contest with "Tediferous", an old Roman word meaning "to bear a torch". Cool.

Funding: it's what makes start-up ventures thrive; it's often what consumes nearly 80% of the time in your initial days. Whether you are preparing for an elevator pitch or a business plan, competitions for the press and prize money they bring, or your investor pitch deck, this process that seems extremely complicated is actually quite simple.

Most people have the image of the American television show "Shark Tank" in their minds when they think of start-ups raising money. Much of this show is theater, but they do give some hints to the actual formula for success.

Often on the show, you will hear the investor moguls beating up the person pitching before them on valuation. You want me to give you how much money, for what percentage of your company? Often, the math doesn't add up. If you have sold $10,000 worth of product, your company is not worth a valuation of $1,000,000. It is as simple as that.

I could go on for days talking about the things that matter in this space. Knowing how to value your company, knowing when the right time is to invest your time trying to gain investors, and knowing when that time does come – how to get the money and most importantly: the right money. It is not easy, and at Rowan University we had just the man to tell us: Howard. The Rowan Innovation Venture Fund (RIVF) was set up for ventures like ours that were standing up in the university and looking for funding. We were in the right place at the right time. So far, this fund had not seen many promising ideas. Our idea was promising, but we – generally speaking – had absolutely no idea what we were doing when it came to pitching.

As engineers who had ventured into the business people's swim lane, we were barely treading water. After months of arduous work building our airtight presentation slide deck and shaking the right hands to get the green light to present before the RIVF, we were courteously given the opportunity to proudly present and casually fail – as 20 or so millionaire investors before us kindly let us know that we were very far from where we needed to be. In retrospect, it made a lot of sense – who were we to say our company had any value at all? Was our value justified with some people coding, a fourth of July beta launch flop, and a trademark filing in progress? No. But, we were lucky enough to have Howard, the RIVF's lead investor, on our side. Realizing that we had potential, he took us under his wing and mentored us over the coming months to refine our pitch and actually stand up the pillars of a company that was worth pitching to investors.

Meanwhile, the Fall semester had drawn to a close. The same Angie who, those four years earlier, had inspired me to pursue the career ambition of spreading international perspective, was herself taking it in by studying abroad in Sao Paulo, Brazil. As I had done for the previous two years, traveling to first study abroad to Germany in 2014, then to visit friends in Germany in 2015, it was again time to travel abroad during that ludicrously long Winter break between Fall and Spring semester, and I was in a plane pointed down toward Brazil to ring in the New Year with Angie. This was a great opportunity to spend some time with my friends, explore, and analyze Brazil to see if it would be a good market in which to launch CultureCloud during the Rio Olympics that upcoming summer of 2016.

It is amazing how quickly things can go from 500 miles per hour to sitting on a couch with your international friend's roommate in Sao Paulo watching an American murder-mystery TV show. Those are the moments that help you settle into truly immersive and cultural experiences. Larissa, Angie's roommate, was incredible, and the next day we boarded a bus together, bound for Rio to meet up with the rest of the group comprised of various international travelers and students from Angie's study abroad program.

After a couple rounds of sightseeing, we went to the supermarket to purchase supplies for the traditional New Year's Eve feast. A couple blocks from Copacabana Beach, everything was normal when we first went into the supermarket, but Brazilian supermarkets are no ordinary affair. Used to the fast-paced sprint of the United States Northeast, the extremely intimate conversations that the checkout employees at the Brazilian supermarket had with every customer were excruciating. They went something along the lines of, "Hello, how are you doing today – how is your family?" *Waits for customer response.* Then after the customer replies in detail, "So great to hear, how are your children?" *BOOP!* as they scan the first item, and this went on and on asking such questions for every item scanned, leading to hour-long wait times to check out.

Walking out of the supermarket near dusk, everything had changed. The small triangle park on the walk back now contained what seemed like 100 Army men setting up a command post, as truck after truck of troops rolled in. While carving out our vodka watermelon, I read online that two million people, sixty thousand military, and five concert stages would line Copacabana Beach that night, bolstered by five barges of fireworks in the middle of the cape and six cruise ships lining the entrance to the cape, encapsulating a celebration of epic proportions.

Sitting around our dinner table making up our crew was me from the US, accompanied by three

Germans, two Columbians, two Mexicans, a girl from China, and a guy from Thailand. This amazingly diverse group was fully prepared in the traditional all-white attire shared by all two million people on the beach. Standing in a circle around our pile of alcohol on the beach, we danced the night away and enjoyed the incredible fireworks display. The fireworks still screaming and exploding above, we popped two bottles of champagne, and as is tradition, stormed the ocean along with thousands around us to jump seven waves for good luck. Nothing has, nor may ever surpass, that surreal experience.

With the parties behind us, we boarded the bus back to Sao Paulo, toured, enjoyed, and relaxed. Then it was off on a 16-hour bus ride to Iguazu Falls. I mention this because it should 100% absolutely be on the bucket list of every traveler to see. For those who have seen Niagara Falls, Iguazu is easily (while not all connected) 10 times as wide as the highest volume waterfall in the world. Brazil offered the panoramic views and Argentina the opportunity to walk in, on, and around the falls. Side note one: do not cross the Brazil/Argentina border on foot. Side note two: do not drink the coffee at the rest stop during the 16-hour bus ride. In my exhausted nature this was the first and only time I made a lapse in the "only drink bottled liquids" rule; it took 15 minutes from coffee to catastrophe and lasted three days.

Why the talk of these amazing Brazil adventures? Because they were just that: adventures. They were not analyzing the market in Brazil as I mentioned in my premise of the trip, and they certainly were not well-utilizing three weeks of free time to grind for my start-up. There is, of course, always room for serendipity, however. Delayed in the Sao Paulo airport awaiting my flight home to Philadelphia, I received a text from a special mentor, Amy. Amy was the kind of mentor who blindly looked out for you, had your back, and always had you in her mind for anything that may pop up that could help you out. That text on January 14th, 2016, was characteristically energetic:

- Amy 3:40 PM: "Hey you!!! So much to catch up on"

- Amy 3:40 PM: "I have a guy I want to do an intro to for you"

- Amy 3:40 PM: "Also developing an app"

- Amy 3:40 PM: "Lots to catch up on"

- Amy 3:40 PM: "Phone call soon??"

I immediately called her via WhatsApp, and a couple of weeks later I was meeting with Matt, the contact she had mentioned, at the Union League in Philadelphia.

Matt too had a start-up venture; only, he had the opposite problem as we did: for the most part, his whole team was business people. Their goal was to build an algorithm that would connect people with the perfect night out, based on local landmarks. Instantly, my IEEE experience came to mind, and I thought to do a quick hackathon. That is, bring in our team to hack away at getting as far as we could with a beta for his team's idea in one solid day of work. In return, it was obvious that Matt's network and expertise would pay off for us.

And so several weeks later we were 30+ floors up in the tallest skyscraper in Philadelphia, laptops up around a conference table, building a beta. Charlie and I worked out user experience stories while the development team built the infrastructure and then eventually began implementation of the basic platform. While we hacked, Matt's team discussed business strategy and casually throughout the day, we had the opportunity to network between teams and build relationships. I had been working for a long time to find ways to bridge the gap between engineers and business people, and it was satisfying to really see this working in a symbiotic way.

Meanwhile, we had gotten good – really good – at pitching CultureCloud as a product. We had a robust business plan to offer. The platform was to be free for users, allowing them to connect based on mutual interests and discover local culture-defining locations they wouldn't find as a tourist. Those businesses we were featuring would pay us a monthly subscription fee for the advertising and receive an analytics report of how many impressions their business was receiving. To make the sales pitch robust, and show we had the global network to launch the platform, we had amassed ten CultureCloud ambassadors from all around the world, who would identify those businesses we would feature with their local knowledge and get a cut of the monthly subscriptions for the businesses they brought on board. What better place to launch this platform than at the Rio Olympics, where millions of international tourists would gather in one place, then travel back home, bringing with them the CultureCloud platform?

Our ask? Angel investor funding to make that summer Rio Olympics launch a reality.

Turns out, we were now ready for the RIVF, and they were very much interested in supporting us. In parallel, our cemented business plan won first place at the Rohrer College of Business plan competition, earning us $10,000 to get started. Plot twist one: another investor we had met was interested. Plot twist two: Matt and his team, inspired by our team and our work during the one-day hackathon for their start-up venture, had decided that rather than pursuing their own project, they wanted to drop it to support us financially.

I had never read so much legal documentation nor met with so many lawyers in my life. Revision after revision and email after email, we locked into three $25,000 convertible note documents (a kind of bond that converts into stock or cash). In parallel, Brad had been admitted into a Carnegie Mellon Ph.D. program that would not allow him to own equity in a start-up venture, so he was to sell his 10% stake for $25,000 across the three investors, making him not only the first person to make money (and a lot of it) from the start-up, but also a lever for the investors to prop up the valuation of the company.

Craziest part – I was in New Zealand. Having graduated, I flew to Kansas to see my grandmom, jumped over to California where I spent time with my German friend, Anna, rented a car and drove down the iconic California Highway 1 to live on a sailboat for a few days, then had jumped over to New Zealand to visit five cities and another great person, Jasleen, whom I had met in Sri Lanka, and eventually would travel to Bali, Indonesia because when I had given my TEDx talk in Bandung, I had been so brazenly scolded for not going to Bali. I say this in one giant sentence because it was as insane as it sounded. Capturing the moment perfectly, I spent eight hours in a Christchurch, New Zealand McDonald's mooching off of their Wi-Fi, carefully documenting the entire financial history of CultureCloud. In Bali, I met the man who commercialized bungie jumping, AJ Hackett, at his five star resort on the Gili Islands, which are the absolute epitome of tropical paradise, and was ripped a freaking new one (that means he was furious) over the phone by Howard from the RIVF when he learned that I was halfway around the globe putzing around.

Unlike the last trip to Brazil, where I thought I would "go down to analyze the market" over Winter break, this time I really did feel as though I was accomplishing a lot. From my McDonald's work sessions to building a social media presence by getting AJ Hackett to sign my CultureCloud t-shirt to actually trending on Twitter with several hundred dolphins on Periscope on the sailboat outside Santa Barbara, I thought I was making progress. In reality, I was wasting time – and a lot of it. At this crucial stage in my start-up, only two months before the Rio Olympics, I needed to be pounding every single moment I had, grinding away at the next steps for the dozens of work threads I knew about, and in doing so, uncovering the work threads I didn't know about. While I was working all day in McDonald's, I was also going on tours and partying. I hung up the phone call from Howard and purchased the fastest flight home I could find.

Having arrived home, I quickly got to work cementing all of the paperwork needed to lock in the convertible notes and Brad's equity transfer.

In parallel, I spun up a contract with a vendor to build in a gamification piece to the app that would allow users to get points for traveling and visiting local partner businesses, as well as see world leaderboards. This was a huge miscalculation. The cost to implement this code with a professional vendor could have funded us on freelance and in-house development for more than a year. The rush job added stress and led to sloppy work as well as the sidelining of other crucial elements that we needed to reach our minimum viable product. Nonetheless, we pushed forward – I even emptied my bank account to make the first down payment and get the work started before we officially got the investment documents signed.

A perfect calculation was partnering with a strategic advertising firm. Understanding our team's weakness, we engaged them to conduct strategic marketing case studies and then a full-fledged advertising campaign for CultureCloud, which was to be supplemented by me and two others on the CultureCloud team on the ground in Rio.

Those weeks ahead of the Rio Olympics were surreal. I was living the legitimate start-up life. I would work in the morning and afternoon and evening and when I should have been sleeping. I would take calls at the gym, and I had no other responsibilities except for the success of the start-up. It was exhilarating.

The choice of who to take to the Olympics with me was easy. Who better to look to than the person who inspired my career ambition in the first place? Angie. Moreover, Angie was now fluent in five languages (although she denies perfecting the languages). The fact that she had been studying in Brazil for six months earlier the same year had added a slew of local contacts and a comprehension of Portuguese to her skillset arsenal. One of her closest friends, Alisa, spoke Spanish, the second-most spoken language in Brazil, and was a natural choice to accompany her.

Their plane tickets were ordered, I attended several meetings with the marketing team, and we conducted twice weekly meetings with the developers we had brought on board. As we approached the Olympics, the CultureCloud-branded sunglasses we ordered arrived, and I stuffed exactly $498 worth into my luggage, which yes, represented 498 pairs of sunglasses, and packed the rest of my things. We finalized a social media ad strategy with the strategic marketing vendor we brought on, and with an absurd amount of confidence, I boarded a flight to Sao Paulo, Brazil for the second time that year.

Notice I forgot something? The app was not fully ready. Our developers were working full throttle to finish the app updates and push to the store as we headed down to Brazil. What's more, Brazilian customs had a "happy" surprise waiting for me when I arrived. For seemingly no other reason than wanting a bribe, they confiscated the sunglasses in my luggage, our primary mechanism for marketing, despite my having the law printed out to show them that allowed me to bring them. The stress of it all collapsed on me, and for the first time in years, I cried.

I finally met up with Angie and Alisa who had been waiting for about two hours, roaming around wondering where I was since I could not use my cell phone in customs. We arrived at the house of an incredible family that was hosting us in the northern area of Rio. They had a great, large apartment with rooftop deck and were incredible to us. Their two daughters, Ana Clara and Mariana, were young, vibrant, friendly, and brimming with excitement to show us their home country. Both attending a German school, they had met Alisa as pen pals – initiating the connection that would eventually bring us together.

While in every other travel story of my life, I really dug into the opportunity to dive into a culture and learn more from those who lived every day in it, this was different. I was in full crisis mode. We needed to urgently order new sunglasses and print out the flyers that we were going to hand out. We had been running social media ads in Rio for two weeks, but the Olympics opening ceremony had happened the night before and we needed to be on the ground, out with the people, building partnerships with hostels and other vendors. We needed to be hustling.

We hit the mall to buy Angie and Alisa matching navy blue shorts and flip flops. Per our marketing partner's direction, it was important to make sure that we all looked the same so that we could be out on the streets representing a cohesive brand; this shopping took a half day. We had the sunglasses ordered and the flyers were picked up; more hours of work. Walking the beaches was absolutely incredible – we had the opportunity to meet some super friendly people who signed our shirts, downloaded the app, and took a picture with us to be posted to social media. Despite this anguish-filled, time-consuming start, we were off and running.

Finally, the new sunglasses arrived. The idea was plain and simple: if you download the app, created a profile, and showed us the app opened to the landing page after profile creation, congratulations, thank you – here is a pair of free CultureCloud-branded sunglasses. They. Were. A. Hit. We would set up shop in varying locations handing out flyers, saying quickly, "Meet people from around the world who share your similar interests!" For those who gave us or the flyer a second glance, we followed up with, "Download the app now for a free pair of sunglasses!" with smiles brimming on our faces.

We were at Copacabana Beach, Ipanema Beach, the Olympic stadiums, just about anywhere you could imagine. If it was a landmark, we made our way there. Since making our way to one of these locations became an afternoon-long activity, we had gotten good at becoming incredibly efficient at stuffing our backpacks full of sunglasses; between the three of us we were able to get 200 sunglasses into our backpacks.

Of all the times we did this, one stood out. Spread out in a line with about five meters between us near a long row of food trucks and displays packed with people, we were handing out flyers. A couple of people began downloading the app, and we would give them sunglasses. Once two or three people were around you, you became a spectacle, and, the curious creatures humans are, people wanted to know what was going on. This particular time we got absolutely mobbed. I have never been in such a wild situation with so many people trying to get my attention at once. Hands reaching over the heads of the hoard surrounding me held out their phone to show me they made it to the CultureCloud landing page. Never seeing their faces, I would reach on my tippy toes above the others to put a pair of sunglasses in their hand. "Five left," I yelled, and there was a relative panic, "Four!" and more frantic pants until finally there were none left. In a period of 20 minutes, we estimated over 300 downloads, the best to date. This really goes to show that you want to pick the best giveaway product for your location. In Rio, that product is sunglasses.

While we went about our promotional activities from day to day, there were always phone calls with the team back home. Some were frustrating. Apple, for instance, was not my biggest friend at the time, nor has it ever been, and it never will be. I hate Apple. Making coding updates to your app and publishing to the app store with Apple in 2016 typically took four to seven days. Despite having published updates to the app through their rigorous review process multiple times before, this time, they decided that our logo looked too similar to the Apple Cloud logo, and we could not publish the app with critical updates needed for the launch until we changed the logo. The very same logo, which was included on all of our branded materials including social media ads, flyers, t-shirts, the website – you name it, everything. Infuriating. Despite multiple initially-tame calls with their customer support, they trended toward ever more vehemently escalated calls with their technical support staff. We gave in to Apple and changed the logo on the Apple app store.

Our social media case studies had come to an end as well. Right when we arrived, we had been offered seven potential ads to run on social media as case studies and were told to pick four to see what our cost per download would be for each. There was one that stood out that we absolutely did not want to pursue. The ad: three girls lying in bikinis on the beach with the caption, "Meet the Locals". For the past year, we had fought to do everything in our power to avoid creating a dating app, but the advisors insisted we run the ad as a baseline to get comparison statistics. Of course, it wildly outperformed the others by more than double. We reluctantly continued to run it.

In parallel, we were able to take advantage of showing Alisa, who had never been to Brazil, the touristy parts along with the sights. Rio de Janeiro is a quintessentially beautiful city, nestled in, on, and around beautiful mountains everywhere, seemingly held into place with the vast ocean, and supported by the warm, orange sky of the breathtaking sunsets. In getting to the best vistas and hitting the classic tourist areas, we were able to take branded photos for our CultureCloud social media page, and they came out very well – despite costing a great deal of time in visiting the sites.

That is one of the most important things to remember about start-ups: really everything takes a lot of time, and time is the biggest thing fighting against you. We had built out a routine of going to a location to give out sunglasses and hand out flyers, visiting hostels to ask them if we could host a pizza party at their location in the evening, heading home to send messages on the app to keep the community thriving, and then heading out to the hostel parties – even a few nights heading out to nightclubs to hand out flyers to those in line.

We got permission to hand out those flyers from the nightclub owner, who was kind enough to help us with another problem we had. One of our goals, perhaps most important, was to throw a launch party in Rio, but we were having trouble finding a location. With the Olympics, the already-hard task of navigating getting a venue in Rio as a foreigner had exponentially increased. Due to a massive amount of unexpected traffic, I missed a meeting with the one venue an existing connection had set up. Yet this nightclub owner was interested in talking about potentially hosting the launch party at one of his venues and growing a partnership beyond the launch party with the app as a whole. So I decided to invest more time in meeting with him; he was a nightclub owner, he worked at night and slept during the day. He missed the meeting. Bitter about the lost couple of hours, I agreed to meet with him again, desperate for a venue. Another skipped meeting, more wasted time.

Luckily, another investment of time had paid off. Despite the hostel parties where we advertised the app being a mix of successful and pretty-much-nobody-showing-up from night to night, one particular owner really took to our initiative, mainly because he loved the product. Rafael was our saving grace. Operating the Maraca Hostel, his location was our first hostel party. He would introduce us to his girlfriend's hostel where we hosted another party, and he would eventually come in clutch by offering Maraca Hostel as the venue for our launch party. Having struggled to lock in the thousands of dollars we expected to need for our launch party, this one only cost us $450 for: the DJ, all-you-can-eat meats, a chef, a bartender, and an open bar for the hundred people that showed up. We sent a notification through the app, messaged those who had downloaded, and spread the word in every way we knew.

This party was the perfect way to cap our time in Rio – it was a huge success. Overall, our time in Rio was not a huge success, though. Of the 10,000 downloads we had hoped to get during our time there, we had achieved 2,500 downloads, which in retrospect was still impressive given the minimum viable product of the coding state of the app and the fact that we had stood up the community in two weeks. Engagement was high, too; although, as time went on, this was proven to be artificial, propped up by our engaging everyone who downloaded the app every evening.

Making our way back to Sao Paulo, I received a notification from Facebook: "Simay is nearby". Simay is a bit of an IEEE legend, having traveled around the world to various events, and she happened to be in Sao Paulo for a convention. We rode together on a hop-on-hop-off bus, and I told her of our past week's effort. Our launch in Rio complete, I spent less than 24 hours on American soil to wash my clothes and head straight to India for the 2016 IEEE conference for members in the Asia-Pacific and Australia region. It was the same congress where I had met Sarang the previous year in Sri Lanka, and it had moved to India for its 50th year celebration.

I gave a talk on entrepreneurship and was again impressed by the sheer excitement and commitment of the IEEE members in attendance. One such member was Amaad, who would eventually become our graphic designer for CultureCloud and who at the time helped me hand out sunglasses and build our CultureCloud user base in India at that conference. It was that same day as I reveled in the Asia-Pacific region's ability to party and dance with absolutely zero alcohol, better than most Western parties I had attended throughout my life, that I overheard one of the organizers of the conference talking about a trip to the Taj Mahal. Shortly after, my friend Nivas tapped me on the shoulder and said briskly, "Hey Jeff – I bought you a plane ticket, I got you a hotel, you owe me money." Twelve hours later, we were on a plane to Delhi.

August 28th is my birthday, and I could not have asked for a better birthday adventure. At 5 AM the next morning, we all piled into the highest-end van we could hire and started pounding the pavement on the way to Agra. In the van was me from the US, a girl from Pakistan, a guy from Iraq, two Indonesian girls, six Japanese guys, and Nivas from India, who had organized the whole trip. It was the epitome of IEEE's global network. We, from all corners of the globe, had come together in that van, road tripping through India, as air conditioner condensation poured from the ceiling, as friends brought together by IEEE on this great journey to one of the Seven Wonders of the World. So surreal was the situation that as Hussain from

Iraq described his pet Mango to the Japanese guys, it was revealed that Mango was a lion – of which he had multiple! The level and greatness of those in that van was beyond measure, and that day is one I will never forget.

I arrived back in the United States after the conference with only days before I was to start my full-time job as a technology consultant; a prestigious position I had attained through a lot of hard work, not knowing if CultureCloud would succeed. It was time to measure that success, and ultimately pit passion against progress. Having been supportive throughout the whole start-up process, I sent an urgent request to my most prestigious mentor, a founder of Priceline.com and patentor of the airport boarding pass kiosk, whom I had cornered at a conference a year earlier to get on the phone and talk through the situation. Stepping away from his father's hospice bed to talk to me on the phone, he said, "If I were you, I wouldn't start that job." I did anyway. After starting my new job, I nevertheless obtained approval to continue growing the CultureCloud community – so long as I did not derive profit.

I often reflect back, wondering if staying with a host family in Rio was a mistake. The rationale and reasoning was solid: save money on housing during this expensive time to be in Rio. Ultimately, the pleasantries of meeting each other and going to visit places was a lot of time utilized when we were there to work, not to be tourists. In the end, Ana Clara and Mariana were an amazing help in connecting us with the sunglasses manufacturer, helping us order the flyers, and helping us set up and execute a launch party, but... I think this was a lesson in translating a passion into a business. When you travel, you take in the culture and engage it; when you run a business, especially launch a business, you spend every living second grinding through those skipped meetings by night club owners, biting your nails in traffic, missing a meeting with a launch party venue owner, and seeking those amazing supporters who let you throw that hostel party at their place for a fraction of the cost. Those cultural and personal connections should have already been built to be leveraged, rather than fostered initially in parallel. We would not have met the Maraca hostel owner for that launch party if it weren't for Mariana and Ana Clara though, and spending tons of time going to the tourist locations to show Alisa around Rio did allow us to relax and build up a strong social media presence.

Everything is a balance. There were tensions between everyone – creating a start-up is stressful work, especially when you have investors who have handed you not only money but trust. The weight of that trust and faith in you is a driver and a burden, a will to succeed and prove that you deserved them, and to give them the satisfaction of being right about choosing your company to invest in. During the start-up launch, I strained my friendship with Angie – she thought that I was disengaged and did not care about our friendship. In a way, she was right – I had deprioritized it in favor of needing to address the business needs of the present, but eventually sat down to explain that and mend relations. Relations were not mended between our iOS and Android developers, though. Austin and Samed had found each other breaking down to yelling at each other on progress and direction. They would eventually catch their cool, rebuild resolve, and push forward through the Olympics, but it ultimately proved to be too much of a load on Austin to proceed at such a pace after the Olympics, and he asked to step away, offering to bring a new lead, Justin, in as the iOS developer.

Having reached only 2,500 of our 10,000 user goal and realizing that maintaining our initial revenue model would be unsustainable, we remembered back to that call with our advertising specialists. They had been right about the girls in bikinis, "Not only have you been able to build a great platform for connecting travelers, but you've actually created a great platform for dating too," they remarked. They were right. We slowly realized that it was more than that, though – we had created a platform for any community to connect in a new way that hadn't been seen before.

IEEE was the perfect example. For years as a Regional Student Representative, I would get requests from volunteer leaders all over the world running all sorts of initiatives asking for volunteers to lead their initiative in the geography I represented. Some of these programs and initiatives I had never heard of before. Even if I had heard of them before, there was no guarantee that I would know anyone who would be able to help by volunteering for their initiative. If I did, I typically only had one or two people in mind.

I thought, "What if all of the IEEE members were featured on the CultureCloud map, and instead of travel filters, the filters were IEEE filters – listing out all of the programs and initiatives in IEEE?" Rather than asking me who was interested in something like the IEEE Xtreme coding competition, a CultureCloud user could filter for "IEEE Xtreme", and instantly everyone would disappear off the map except for those interested in that program. This would be a powerful platform to create instant connection to everyone who could be your potential volunteer leader, and as an administrator, you could push a notification to all of those users about relevant updates to their interests.

Moreover, IEEE hosts more than 1,800 conferences every year around the globe. What if we featured all of those on the map as well, including speakers, bios, the ability to ask questions, logistics, etc.? Doing so would allow for post-event engagement as well. We had the same basic functionality of all other conference apps out there, but instead of focusing on one event you could find all of them and show all the members the power of the network. This was the only conference platform that would allow you to pay for and feature not one event, but a community of your events and members. While IEEE was a familiar conduit through which to explain it, any organization or professional society could derive value from it. And so: pivot, CultureCloud Community mode was born.

Action Items Related to Chapter Nine

1. Learn your Myers-Briggs personality type. Has it surprised you about your personality? Analyze how knowing your personality type can be leveraged to make the teams you are in more effective.

2. List three of your most cherished or strongly held opinions. What has made you strongly believe them? Try to persuade yourself to change your mind. Do you think it is logical that society as a whole should agree with you? Why?

3. Earn $20 doing something that is not your normal job or skill set.

4. Ponder an idea for a business. Research the competitors. Assess whether you can make a better product. Think of who in your network you would invite to your team to make it full of diverse skill sets if you were to launch the business.

Jeffrey Eker Jr. & Sarang Shaikh

10: LIVING GLOBALIZED

Lesson: Always recognize and appreciate the privilege of your situation.

British secret agent operative turned author, Somerset Maugham, wrote a book in 1944 titled *The Razor's Edge*, which follows the life of a fellow named Larry. After choosing to "loaf" on the financial support of his inheritance rather than working a job, Larry forgoes his marital engagement, leaving behind his fiancée to seek happiness in life – by trying to discover what made him happy at a foundational level. He travels through Europe, from one adventure to the next. Eventually, he comes to learn that his fiancée has chosen another who gives her a debonair lifestyle. Larry then also faces tragedy as he learns that his childhood friend, whom he admired greatly and maintained a serene memory of from their younger days, had died from a lifestyle of drug and alcohol addiction.

Multiple times throughout the novel, Larry has the opportunity to return to what is considered a typical lifestyle with a "normal" job. Yet, he moves from job to job and country to country in a nomadic pilgrimage to experience life, hardship, and people of varying cultures. Every step of the way, life itself seems to become more straightforward while the definition of happiness becomes more complex.

Eventually, Larry sits atop a mountain in India and determines that, after his long journey, he has found happiness through nature and spirituality. He returns back to America, gets a normal job, and becomes complacent in having discovered happiness. This abrupt decision of having achieved happiness, despite the novel's constant reminder of the complexity of its definition, begs the questions: can happiness be found by simply achieving fulfillment in life? What is fulfillment? For Larry, this very well could have been that he was satisfied in the execution of his quest.

We may not ask ourselves these questions daily, but if you are conscious of your personal journey toward happiness and fulfillment, you may realize just how much you take for granted and just how much more you can achieve.

In December of 2017, Sarang and I were walking through the streets of Washington, D.C., heading toward a pitch for CultureCloud that would have nationwide potential. I was incredibly sick with some type of flu-like illness that had me feeling worse than I had in years. Fighting to overcome the symptoms enough to execute the pitch, I quietly engaged Sarang in conversation so as to avoid straining what little was left of my voice that I was mustering for the presentation.

For Sarang, this might as well have been the equivalent of Armageddon. For a guy from Pakistan, where swelteringly hot days were the norm and air conditioning sometimes a luxury, the fact that we had dropped far below a freezing ambient temperature and were currently barreling through gusty, wind-filled streets was torture. No number of jackets would suffice.

As we both shivered, resolutely marching the six blocks from our accommodations to the pitch, I remembered that Sarang's birthday was coming. As cordially as my sickness would allow, I pitifully exclaimed, "Sarang – your birthday is coming up!" followed by, "What are you going to do to celebrate?!" His reply was less than exciting.

"I don't celebrate my birthday," he replied, pausing lightly. "For the past several years I have had nothing to celebrate," he said, going on to elaborate that over the past several years he had gone to many start-up pitches just like this one and seen many start-ups he was assisting fail. Finally, he sighed, resolutely with an unmoved expression, "so I don't celebrate at all."

This was absolutely shocking to me – I had not heard something so depressing in years. At a minimum, I pushed, "You have to at least celebrate all of the great parts about friends and being able to travel." But the mindset was cemented, and there wasn't much room to change Sarang's thought process. In fact, he was beginning to convince me, too.

We arrived at our destination. The pitch could not have gone worse, except for the fact that most people aren't so candid in letting you down.

A Sarang-coined term, "lollipop promises" are agreements to get you to smile as you leave, with perhaps a smidge of false hope, like when a doctor gives you a lollipop to walk out of their office smiling. All too often, especially in American culture, this is very common when pitching in any scenario. That day we were at least happy to roll out with a resolute "no" and a couple of next steps that might help us get closer to the same solar system as the "yes" we were looking for. We walked somberly out of the office, focused on the misfortune of the day.

Walking through DC that day exploring, I got a call on my cell phone. My dad had called to let me know that we received our first form of revenue for CultureCloud – a $1,000 check! Later that day, Sarang received news that he was one of 20, among thousands of applicants around the world, to be accepted into a prestigious fellowship program. We were reminded that everything wasn't terrible after all.

The whole reason we were in DC was due to a conference that Sarang had found online a couple of months back, the World Bank Youth Summit. Completely oblivious to the immense power of the World Bank, I thought, "Okay, this looks cool – I'll apply." Sarang and I were both accepted to attend and had made plans to travel to DC to attend.

It turns out that the only other person to sit in on all G20 meetings, aside from the Presidents of those G20 countries, is the President of the World Bank. The World Bank is an organization that funds the development of emerging nations as an international consortium. Of the 400 attendees at the World Bank Youth Summit, over 100 countries were represented – meaning it was an incredible privilege to attend this gathering of leaders under 30 years old from around the world. To think I had initially applied on a whim because I had thought, "Well, this looks cool."

It was cool – really cool. By the end of the conference, both Sarang and I had made some incredible connections, enjoyed powerful talks, and walked out with lifelong friends. Having started the trip incredibly sullen, I said goodbye to Sarang on a dance floor (as he tore it up) much happier and fulfilled. We both had an understanding and a course correction. We were indeed, despite the many challenges we faced in our current endeavors, very privileged to be where we were in life: in a bar on the second floor, dancing the night away with youth leaders from over 100 countries. When we weren't happy, we were fulfilled by the pursuit of our mission; and when we were happy, it was typically hanging out with incredible people from all around the world – fulfillment would be pursued again tomorrow.

This final chapter we are leaving you with is written from my (Jeff's) voice, but know these words come written in collaboration and directly from both of us and our passion. It was a mere four hours after that initial pitch that we sat together in a sprawling DC cafeteria and devised the idea for this book. We did so with the idea and intention to emphasize that we had taken so much of where we were in life for granted, and sometimes we needed reminders – jolting us to return to being incredibly appreciative of our situation and standing in life.

The fact of the matter is: you, wherever you are in the world, have the tools to do the same. While there is always a bit of luck in any good storyline, it always arises out of some form of determination. In our globalized world today, wielding the digital tools, networks, and relationships that society has provided us, anyone can achieve a positive impact on a worldwide level. Is it easy? Absolutely not. You require first a passion, then a project, some hard work, and the little pieces of luck you'll find along the way.

We did it, we continue to do it, and we know that you can, too. If you don't believe us, here are some stories from others who are Living Globalized to guide you on your journey along the way.

Action Items Related to Chapter Ten

1. Watch the documentary "Bending the Arc" about the World Bank President during the time Living Globalized was written.

2. Reach out to a friend who lives outside your country or far away that you rarely see. Thank them for an impact that they have made on your life through a story of their providing outside perspective.

Part Three

Friends' Stories

The following stories have been compiled with a simple prompt: "What is your most impactful international story?"

These stories were generated by 22 people, coming from 10 countries, discussing their travels across 40 countries. We asked our friends and mentors to let us know their stories to help you frame what yours might become. Reflecting the individuality and building on the unique identities of the wide swath of people we reached out to, note that some of the stories fit snugly into the 300-word limit we prescribed, some people wrote very serious stories, and some wrote quirky travel stories. Every one of these authors is just another person, just like you, who is following their passion.

We hope you enjoy these capstone stories. Thank you to everyone who contributed their stories to be published alongside our own. We would also like to thank Alef Carloto for the incredible cartoon drawings throughout. The final shows a map of the countries referenced in Living Globalized – both throughout the book and in the stories that follow.

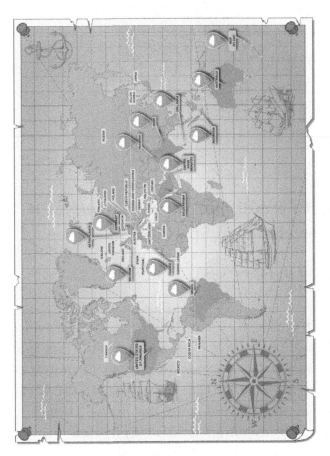

Abir Chermiti, Software Engineer & ICT for Development Specialist

Country in Story: USA

I don't know if I can call myself a traveler because I don't have a long list of countries that I've visited. My passion for travel is new; two years ago I first got the chance to "see the world from the small window of the plane". I was 21 years old traveling for the first time to the United States. I know for some of you it's late at this age, but it's different in every culture. Where I come from, it's new for a very young girl to travel ALONE to a very far place.

I was so crazy about my first trip to California in the USA that, when I left my final exams to go, I cannot deny that I was afraid about the risks I was about to take on and the fact that I would need to take full responsibility of everything that was about to come next.

Facing that fear, I remember that I was not alone. I was surrounded by people, even those I had never met in real life, people who inspired me and supported me in my decisions. One of them told me, "sometimes we have to risk for what we really want to do - if you want to be in California, go! You don't know what doors this will open for you there", and she was right!

That trip opened a new chapter in my whole life; it made me the person I am today, I met my virtual friends for the very first time, and I made new friends, with whom I am still connected today, trying to catch any opportunity to meet around the world. Many of them invited me to their countries (India, USA, UAE, Kenya, Morocco, etc.) and I invited them to my country (Tunisia), as well. I even developed projects with some of them, and we worked together to organize many events.

Traveling has always been a very beautiful experience in my life. It has never been very easy to do it, but when I do, I get the feeling that I am FREE, in the air, and meeting people that I know will become lifetime treasures.

I'm grateful for the risks I took and the people I got to know, and I'm sure that my life couldn't be better without having you – my friends, wherever you are on this beautiful earth, I'm sending you my love.

AJ Winkler, Chief Executive Officer - Kolu, Inc

Country in Story: Japan

I sit here in Osaka International Airport waiting to board my flight to Seoul. I cannot help but to think back on my exploration of Japan. Just like any trip, this one made me feel a multitude of emotions. It was an incredible journey that I will not be able to fully digest for months to come.

Throughout my travels of over 25 countries, I've always felt a degree of cultural shock at times, but usually embrace the feeling. In preparation for this trip, I read up on the culture, took Japanese lessons, reached out to alumni, and watched countless YouTube videos. On this trip I felt something unique that I could not quite pinpoint until writing this story. There had been feelings of melancholy, jubilance, fascination, confusion, and frustration. My time in Japan was encapsulated in one feeling - cultural dissonance. From the moment that I arrived seeing countless unhappy salarymen in the metro to the immaculate streets (sidenote: there were no trash cans – at all); Japan felt like a 180-degree switch from the United States. To better understand without traveling to Japan, check out the movie Lost in Translation. Moreover, it serves as a viewpoint of an American traveling to Japan that feels more than just being out of place. Even though the movie is 15 years old, it is still very relevant.

Consequently, I kept imagining what my experience would have been if my company, Kolu, had operations in Japan so visitors could receive a truly authentic experience. The Japanese population is a homogeneous group, even more so in comparison to countries in Europe. I can only imagine someone going to Japan for business or leisure being overwhelmed. Breaking the cultural and language barrier that exists in Japan can be quite a challenge, but well worth the reward.

Amaad Soomro, Graphic Designer

Countries in Story: Pakistan and the United States

"Travel is the bridge between you and everything." ~ Rumi

Born in a small village in a rural area of Pakistan that doesn't even exist on Google Maps, I had never imagined that I would be traveling around the world. It was my passion for technology and design that promised me amazing opportunities to do so.

I grew up in a society that is conservative about embracing different cultures and sects have a huge negative impact on cultural sensitivity. When I started meeting different people around the world through travel, I learned one thing which completely changed how I see the world. No matter which culture you're from or what religion you follow, you're essentially a human like any other on the planet.

I was heading to California on my first ever international trip to attend a conference and I had to collect my room keys from the host soon after I landed in San Francisco. I was enjoying my in-flight Wi-Fi around 35,000ft over the mountains, when I received a message from my friend who was to pick me up, that he wouldn't be able to come due to a family medical emergency. I started searching for the best options available and booked a shuttle while still in the sky. When walking out of the airport, I heard a guy calling my name at the bus stop and I was able to quickly catch the ride without making any delay. So you never know what's going to crop up when you travel but digital tools are always there to rescue.

I love how traveling opens new ways to gain learning, opportunities, and most importantly valuable connections. This is clear that with the internet and digital tools, we are globalizing quickly.

I never want to stop learning and connecting with people from all over.

Amir Zahoor

Countries in Story: Sweden, Estonia, Russia, and Finland

Occurring in March 2012, this amazing journey is the true experience of the Baltic Sea and the surrounding countries. The Baltic Sea is a marginal sea of the Atlantic Ocean, enclosed by Finland, Sweden, Denmark, Estonia, Latvia, Lithuania, Russia, Poland, Germany and the North and Central European Plain. We traveled the St. Peter Line on a journey starting from Stockholm, Sweden.

Day 1 – Stockholm (Sweden) | Departure: 5:30pm

I, along with my university fellows, started our 5 days trip from Stockholm, Sweden. Old Town or Gamla Stan of Stockholm is filled with beautiful houses and cozy little squares, but its history is ripe with blood-chilling stories. We enjoyed The Royal Palace, the St. George and the Dragon statue, and Stockholm Cathedral.

Sweden is a Scandinavian nation with thousands of coastal islands and inland lakes, along with vast boreal forests and glaciated mountains. Stockholm, the capital of Sweden, encompasses 14 islands and more than 50 bridges on an extensive Baltic Sea archipelago. The cobblestone streets and ochre-colored buildings of Gamla Stan (the old town) are home to the 13th-century Storkyrkan Cathedral, the

Kungliga Slottet Royal Palace, and the Nobel Museum, which focuses on the Nobel Prize. Ferries and sightseeing boats shuttle passengers between the islands.

Day 2 – Tallinn (Estonia) | Arrival: 12:30pm | Departure: 6:30pm

We spent day 2 in Tallinn. We were taken on a Tallinn city trip led by a local guide where you spend time seeing all of its famous sights: Tallinn's Famous Churches, Freedom Square, Kiek in de Kök, Danish King's, Garden, Toompea, Alexander Nevsky Cathedral, Viewpoints, Tallinn Town Hall Square, Old Tallinn City Wall, and Harju Street.

Estonia, a country in Northern Europe, borders the Baltic Sea and Gulf of Finland. Including more than 1,500 islands, its diverse terrain spans rocky beaches, old-growth forest and many lakes. Tallinn, Estonia's capital on the Baltic Sea, is the country's cultural hub. It retains its walled, cobblestoned Old Town, home to cafes and shops, as well as Kiek in de Kök, a 15th-century defensive tower. Its Gothic Town Hall, built in the 13th century and with a 64m-high tower, sits in historic Tallinn's main square. St. Nicholas Church is a 13th-century landmark exhibiting ecclesiastical art.

Day 3 – St. Petersburg (Russia) | Arrival: 9:00am | Departure: 6:00pm

We spent day 3 in St. Petersburg, Russia! Millions of visitors come every year to admire this beautiful city. It is hard to imagine that all the palaces and magnificent buildings were built within only a few decades. The northernmost megacity of the world is a UNESCO World Heritage Site and the most important port of Russia. A shuttle bus takes you to downtown St. Petersburg and in the afternoon back to the port.

Russia, the world's largest nation, borders European and Asian countries as well as the Pacific and Arctic oceans. Its landscape ranges from tundra and forests to subtropical beaches. St. Petersburg is a Russian port city on the Baltic Sea. It was the imperial capital for 2 centuries, having been founded in 1703 by Peter the Great, the subject of the city's iconic "Bronze Horseman" statue. It remains Russia's cultural center, with venues such as the Mariinsky Theatre hosting opera and ballet, and the State Russian Museum showcasing Russian art, from Orthodox icon paintings to Kandinsky works.

Day 4 – Helsinki (Finland) | Arrival: 9:00am | Departure: 6:00pm

We spent day 4 in Helsinki to discover the major attractions such as the Uspenski Cathedral, the Helsinki Cathedral, the Suomenlima, or admire the island Seurasaari in the middle of the Finnish capital. In Helsinki, there are also many museums and galleries that are well worth a visit.

Finland is a Northern European nation bordering Sweden, Norway and Russia. Its capital, Helsinki, occupies a peninsula and surrounding islands in the Baltic Sea. Helsinki is home to the 18th-century sea fortress Suomenlinna, the fashionable Design District, and diverse museums. The Northern Lights can be seen from the country's Arctic Lapland province, a vast wilderness with national parks, ski resorts, imposing Parliament House, and Kiasma, a contemporary art museum. Ornate red-brick Uspenski Cathedral overlooks a harbor.

Day 5 – Stockholm (Sweden) | Arrival: 07:00am

We returned back to Stockholm in the morning of day 5. That was a truly memorable 5-days trip to Sweden (Stockholm), Estonia (Tallinn), Russia (St. Petersburg) and Finland (Helsinki).

Andrew Holtz, Project Manager at Kairos GmbH

Countries in Story: Germany and Sierra Leone

This is a story of how I joined a German family while living in Bo, Sierra Leone during the summer of 2017.

The semester before finishing my bachelor's degree at Middlebury College, I made the decision to live in Sierra Leone for an extended period of time before moving to Berlin, Germany. The woman that raised me, who I now call my mother, has been living in Sierra Leone since 2010, and I wished to spend time with her in her home country. With a background in molecular biology, I went to Sierra Leone to work for the U.S. Naval Research Lab in Bo, Sierra Leone to teach and implement modern techniques for detecting infectious diseases.

The first couple of weeks in country, I integrated myself into Sierra Leone culture. I befriended the lab technicians, and I found individuals in the community to practice my Krio with. I reconnected with the foods and language from my childhood. At the end of my third week, I learned of a German family that lived close by. Little did I know at this point, how beneficial my experience in Germany, and in the German language, would be in rural Sierra Leone. I slowly started visiting the family, sharing stories of our daily encounters. I was accepted into this new network and taken in as one of their own. As the weeks passed, heading to their house for dinner, a movie, or discussions became routine. Who would have guessed that in the middle of rural West Africa, I would once again find comfort thanks to the German language? As a coincidence, the family was from Berlin, so when it came to finding an apartment for my Fulbright Scholarship in Berlin, they were able to instruct me. One of the individuals from the house moved back to Berlin, and we now meet often in the city for coffee.

This experience was only possible because of the privilege I have been given. I am privileged to know the importance of learning a foreign language. I am privileged as an educated, white, male graduate of a liberal arts college. I am privileged for the opportunities to participate in international exchanges in high school. I am privileged to have been exposed to other cultures, languages, and food through my mother. I am privileged for the financial state of my family, which allowed me to travel. I took advantage of these privileges to place myself on a global scale.

Angelika Hom, Masters Student

Countries in Story: Brazil and Germany

"We keep moving forward, opening new doors, and doing new things, because we're curious and curiosity keeps leading us down new paths." ~ Walt Disney

For one last time I sat on that bench in the beautiful heart of São Paulo, in a seat I had frequented to relax in a city that I had called home for six months. It was the last time I was observing the people passing by me, trying to guess where they came from and what they have gone through in life. This was the time when I began to recall my whole semester abroad in Brazil and the moment when I suddenly remembered the inspiring moments from my journey.

Before I started my semester abroad in Brazil, everyone back in Germany was puzzled because of my decision to spend six months in, what was in their eyes, one of the most dangerous countries in our world today. This reaction caused a slight feeling of discomfort in me that surprisingly vanished as soon as I spent my first day in São Paulo. I can proudly say that my time in Brazil was so far the most enriching experience in my life. This experience has taught me to approach a new country with curiosity, interest, empathy, and an openness of the mind instead of being led by old prejudices. With this in mind, I had the chance to get to know the most amazing people, explore one of the most beautiful countries of our world, and embrace a completely new culture. My semester abroad definitely shaped my character and personality, empowering me to move forward and explore new paths whenever I get the chance.

You do not have to travel to the other side of the world to experience that feeling. Just take your chance wherever you are and start exploring the beauty that our world offers!

Ayat Mohammad Mahmoud, Computer Engineer

Countries in Story: Jordan, Palestine, USA, Dubai, Tunisia, and UK

I grew up watching the young Jordanian women around me marry early and abandon their studies. Still, I always worked hard in high school to get good grades. I hoped for a scholarship. I started creating opportunities for myself. I didn't blame my family's financial situation. I was offered a Microsoft internship in Germany. The IEEE Students and Young Professional Congress for Europe, Africa, and the Middle East that year happened to be in Poland, and I thought I'd be able to attend the event while working at my internship. But I almost didn't go. I went to my father and I told him that I wanted to travel to Europe and he said, "No dear, you won't. None of our girls travel outside and you also want to travel alone. That's a dream." I tried my best to convince him but he kept saying, "NO", so I came up with a solution. I secured funding for my father to travel along with me as my chaperone and my father borrowed the rest. After that, he felt that he could give me more trust and he was ready now to fight...to help his daughter pursue her future.

Since then, the world has opened up to me. With my father's blessing, I attended the FLL Competition in St. Louis, Missouri, in 2015, interned at NASA Johnson Space Center in Houston, Texas, and attended the Women in Engineering International Leadership Conference (WIE ILC) 2016 in San Jose, California.

Attending the WIE ILC turned out to be one of the most amazing experiences in my life. I was surrounded by creative and talented women from all over the world who have made a difference working at large companies like Cisco, Intel, Facebook, and Google. The sheer privilege of having the ability to be in the same room as them and engage them in conversation was astounding. Whenever I look at each of these role models, I like to try to imagine myself where they are after ten years, learning what they have already learned, experiencing everything they have been through, and being able to talk about it freely with like-minded individuals. Traveling taught me a lot. Traveling is an opportunity where differences in politics, ethnicity, personalities, attitudes, and dreams can come together to create something beautiful: harmony.

Charlie W. Grab, Account Manager

Country in Story: Italy

I was in Rome with two of my best friends from University, living in the attic of the one friend's sister's apartment. She was dating a boxing coach, and during one of our chats with him, it was mentioned that I was once a wrestler. Right away he said he would like to host us to a day at his boxing gym, and though none of us had ever boxed before, we were pumped to go and said, "absolutely".

The very next day, we're at the boxing gym: nervously excited and confused. This confusion came from a combination of our nerves and a sizeable language barrier; no one was speaking

English in this gym. We began a group practice session and played follow-the-leader to keep up during the mostly aerobic exercise. Things got interesting once the practice wrapped up.

As we're walking back to the entrance, we were greeted by our host and a sizable crew of burly combat men. One of these men, who most nearly resembled a 5-foot, 8-inch cement block, stepped forward and shook my hand while nodding his head towards me and saying something in Italian. I looked over to our host in confusion, and he said something along the lines of: "this man was the Italian silver medalist in grappling and would like to wrestle you."

Even though I am 6-foot, 2-inches and likely had 30lbs on the man, I was immediately nervous... what had I gotten myself into? So I looked around the gym for a wrestling mat (we were currently all standing on hardwood flooring), but didn't see one. I looked back to the cement block and tried communicating that I would wrestle him, but I didn't see where. He responded by stepping closer to me and making a repeated gesture of reaching for my legs while saying "wrestle", smiling and looking me in the eye between each statement of the word. So, right there on the hardwood floor while surrounded by about 15 people, I tackled the man.

What followed was a battle on the hardwood floor that eventually resulted in me pinning this cement block man to a roar of cheers from the crowd. Both of us hopped to our feet, and despite only being able to communicate the word "wrestle" between us verbally, we shared a hug that said, "man, I don't know what just happened, but that was awesome. You're awesome."

Christopher Gwin, Instructor of German Language Courses

Countries in Story: USA and Germany

I have believed in the power of connection during my entire career. There is a joy and a source of great strength in bringing people together across the world, and I have striven to make this joy possible for as many people as possible. At the base level, we are humans and when we make these connections, we deepen our capacity to be human and to share the world more equitably and more sustainably.

I started my career teaching German the year the wall fell, 1989. In the freshmen German One class sat Joanna Richards, who stood out because she demonstrated a sincere and rather keen interest in learning the language, and for her intellect and her sense of worldliness. After one year, I took a position closer to Philadelphia and had sparse contact with Joanna after that year.

More than 20 years later, I was at the Leibnizschule in Wiesbaden, Germany for our first exchange with that school. We arrived on the last day of school and I attended the teacher farewell barbecue. The partner teacher, Moni, mentioned that there was a sports teacher she wanted me to meet. I could not understand why she wanted to do this, as I have no interest in sports. She kept mentioning this as the hours passed. She also mentioned that his wife was American. Finally, they arrived and as I turned to be introduced to Raoul, I screamed – loudly! very loudly – and Joanna screamed! We had not seen each other in twenty years, but there she was attending the party with her husband, the sports teacher Moni wanted me to meet, who could never have known the history between us! This is a moment in which everyone says: "what a small world!"- and this is the miracle of human connection.

Now, I have regular communication with Joanna, know her children, and spend time with them when I am in Wiesbaden or when they are in New Jersey. Joanna has studied and lived in various places in the world, choosing to raise her family in Germany, which is a source of great joy for me.

Gina Tierno, Freelancer

Country in Story: Japan

I used to say I liked to travel alone. But looking back on my adventures, I never was alone. I thought I had developed the art of meeting people, but actually, I was cultivating a different skill entirely. It was the skill of "the ask". It was a two-part method: 1) what to ask and 2) how to ask.

I always made it a point when traveling somewhere new to make a list of things I wanted to accomplish, see, and eat. This makes it easy to answer the question: "what brings you to <insert foreign country here>"? It not only makes carrying on a conversation with even the most awkward people bearable but satisfies point one in the "ask for it" method.

Now for part two. Making "the ask" flow naturally. I started making a habit of asking people if they knew anyone either in the country or that had traveled there. This is where I found the networking "6 degrees of separation" really shows its truth. The people I spoke to would connect me to a colleague who introduced me to their friend who has a family member who studied with a person that would eventually become my new best friend. And this is how I climbed the summit of Mount Fuji.

I was twenty at the time when I found myself on an 18-hour flight to Tokyo. I was beginning a new life in a new world without knowing anyone or the language. It was from a simple mentioning of how I wanted to climb the 12,395 ft mountain that I was put in touch with a complete stranger who would instruct me on how to climb the snow-topped mountain.

We met over bottles of Asahis where he looked me up and down and admitted that he wasn't sure my 4-foot, 11-inch frame could handle the climb. I insisted I was going to try. After he recounted his previous climb over a few pints, I realized I was unaware of the physical strength and supplies needed to climb the mountain. I reluctantly I told him I couldn't afford the supplies to complete such a feat. We parted ways.

He messaged me three days later. He had bought me brand new hiking boots that I still wear to this day. He lent me an extra hiking backpack, trekking poles, and provided me with external winter clothing. Most importantly, he told me, with the purest intentions, that he was going to accompany me to the summit.

I'm not sure if I ever would have successfully made it up that mountain if it wasn't for him. There were a lot of times where he caught me from falling or gave me a boost to the next rock ledge. The compassion of other cultures for travelers continues to astound me as I travel. I have countless stories about how the Japanese take such pride in their country. They seem to take it upon themselves that you have a good experience in their country. It seems like a ridiculous thing to do for your country, but not a day goes by where someone mentions Japan and I don't recall the hospitable nature of my lifelong friends.

J. N. Alexander, Teacher

Countries in Story: Iceland and the Semi-Autonomous Free-State of Grimsey Island

Many people are under the assumption when they travel that the trip itself is the adventure and as such that something great will simply happen across them or perhaps they will be able to suddenly examine the world through a new lens. However, this is not the case. The adventure, connections, and perspectives that travel can give us mean nothing until we take charge of our own destiny. Indeed, many a person go through life expecting great things to be bestowed upon them, only to feel jaded, as what they thought would be a full life comes to a rapid close, and they realize that they are just nearly spent shells.

Therefore, for our own sake, we must delineate between the concepts of travel and adventure. Travel is defined in the previous paragraph as the mere act of going somewhere. It puts us in the physical location of the human experience, but it does not give us experience. It cannot give us a deeper understanding of ourselves or the world around us. Adventure, however, gives us the unique opportunity to breathe, eat, walk, and stumble upon the human experience against the backdrop of new worlds. This is because it considers not just the action of going, but how one goes.

One of my favorite adventures comes from an unassuming island, Grimsey, which is about a three-hour ferry ride off of the coast of Iceland. Grimsey's main claim to fame is that a small portion of the island falls within the Arctic Circle. As a matter of a fact, that simple item led some of my friends and I to make the decision to go there. Now, traveling to Iceland, sailing way out into the North Sea, or even going into the Arctic Circle are pretty neat. Any one or any combination of those items would certainly be welcome additions to any traveler's resume. Yet, simply doing any of those things really does not have a lot of value or importance. Anyone can go to Google Images and find pictures of what we saw or physically go to where we were, if they possess the means. It is the fact that we turned that trip into an adventure that made Grimsey a memory for the ages.

Instead of allowing a six-hour round trip ferry ride on a cold, grey, cloudy day to be a drag, we took the time to realize the ridiculousness of our situation as this trip turned from travel into an adventure. Our ridiculous situation was first underlined by the informational video for tourists that our ferry captain played for us. The video must have been made by the inhabitants of the island in the 1980s or 90s. As one might imagine, an island with the population of a poorly attended 4th of July barbecue party did not have the cinematic resources or experiences of Hollywood. So this video ran like a stream of conscious as different islanders added bits and bits to the fabled history of Grimsey. It contemplated everything from the island's history to its economy, to its possible secession from Iceland, to things a tourist cannot miss. The contents of this video helped us to form the necessary mindset needed to really enjoy everything that this strange island had to offer. This meant that we walked all over the island which led us to discover things like a giant concrete ball, which they referred to as a sculpture. We saw a highly complex inter-island trade go down which involved trading a burned-out car for a dumpster (the mainland definitely got the better end of the trade, in my opinion). We indeed went into the Arctic Circle, where we played with puffins and seagulls. We were able to walk on the esteemed island golf course, which was a semi-mowed 100 yard strip with holes on both ends and no flags. We played soccer on the soccer field, where I scored a goal (you can call me the Pele of the north). As we returned to the more developed part of the island, we made sure to pick up an Arctic Circle certificate from the dual gift shop and three-room hotel. All of that exploring made us quite peckish, which resulted in us having the opportunity to have the distinct pleasure of eating lunch at the restaurant on the island, which was named "The Restaurant".

Unfortunately, the chef informed us that we did not have enough time from him to catch then serve us the island's specialty, puffin. After that meal, we went to the store, which, you guessed it, was named "The Store", where we bought the island out of cookies. The Store was not happy about that. Then as we waited for the ferry, we played chess on this harbor overlook which provided way too beautiful of a backdrop for people to eat cookies and play chess. Finally, we enjoyed talking to Icelandic school children and trading snacks as we watched the movie Madagascar on the return trip.

This story would not have been possible without our willingness to turn our situation into something more than it was. If this had been a mere trip, it most likely would have been a wash because in reality this was a small island in the middle of nowhere, on a cold, rainy day, with not a lot to do. However, since this was an adventure, we were able to overlook the physical realities of the situation in order to really enjoy this moment as we ate, drank, and walked all over it. As a result, we had the benefit of gaining a small glimpse into the world of people no one would think about and formed a closer bond between ourselves. Personally, this experience was one of the crowning moments of my trip to Iceland because it gave me such an incredible opportunity to really experience what the soul of the country is, fundamentally: both honest and hardworking, yet completely absurd.

Jasleen Kaur, Engineer

Countries in Story: America, India, Pakistan, Sri Lanka, New Zealand, Australia

Rewind back 4 years - An Indian living in New Zealand at the time (Jasleen) attends a conference in Sri Lanka. There she meets an American and a Pakistani delegate (Jeff and Sarang).

Fast forward 4 years - Jasleen now lives in Australia and just got back from a holiday in America and Canada (June to July 2018)!

One of my colleagues, on the last day before their retirement, said this to me: go on adventures, because adventures give you stories, and stories connect you to the world. And if there is one thing that all my travel adventures to date have been, it is a beautiful collection of memorable stories.

I am blessed to have traveled to a few parts of the world that have given me friendships that I know will last forever, memories that I will never forget, taught me things that I did not think were important, and made me a person I never imagined I would become.

So if you ever get a chance to explore, experience and learn from the world of people around you, and you are unsure, do it for the story. You never know, you might end up sharing your story in a book of someone you meet in some part of the world. The reason why I am a part of this book is because I once caught a flight to Sri Lanka and ended up meeting Jeff and Sarang.

Life fact: since I met Jeff 4 yours ago, we have managed to meet in a different part of the world every year. Four years, four countries – and counting!

Jeffrey Eker, Mechanical Engineer

Countries in Story: United States and the World's Oceans

In 1983, I circumnavigated the globe during a 125-day voyage aboard a cargo ship. This was part of my Marine Engineering course of instruction while I was a Midshipman at the United States Merchant Marine Academy. I was 21 years old and the internet, let alone the Internet of Things (IoT), were not yet a part of the everyday world. However, as a result of this

125-day experience where I visited ports and interacted with people from numerous cultures, I was Living Globalized. For perspective, my children did not have cell phones until about 2004 when the oldest, Jeffrey, was in fourth grade (smart phones were not widely used until several years later). One of my roommates in college was the smartest engineer in the class. Nicknamed "Flash", he purchased a personal computer (PC) during our senior year. PCs were not introduced into the workplace until a few years later, and it was typical for one PC to be shared by ten people.

Hence my initial experiences of Living Globalized came about as a result of my schooling, which was related to and driven by international trade, commerce, governance, and geo-political concerns. The seemingly endless modernization, mechanization, and computerization of what began to accelerate during the industrial revolution enabled my globalization and has also evolved to the newest innovations, including the IoT, Bio-Medical Engineering, and James Web Space Telescope just to name a few. It is interesting to note that my initiation to Living Globalized began while in school, and it was likewise for my son. While some of our early involvements in Living

Globalized were engineering related, his quickly progressed to much more than that by utilizing modern technology, communications, and innovations, as is evidenced in this book.

I could go on about how I tried to enlighten my children about the 'you can do anything, you can be anything' ideals that all parents attempt to impart to their children (my favorite was my rants on string theory and time measurements), but as time goes on I realize that I was just a relatively small, but essential part of what is happening now. So, while Living Globalized is a very, very real marvel, and living universalized or living beyond universalized may be being realized, the existential priority is possibly to apply this phenomenon – in order to adjudge monumental outcomes. So, if you were ever wondering whence the apples fell....

Jim Jefferies, 2018 IEEE President

Countries in Story: Many

An International Experience ~ Jim Jefferies

Sometimes an event or experience changes perspective or permanently reinforces a view in a way that only a personal experience can provide. For me, such an event occurred in Regensburg, Germany in 2016 when I was campaigning for the office of President-elect of IEEE.

The event was the biannual gathering of young professionals and students from across Europe, the Middle East, and Africa regions. Over the course of several days, I met, heard experiences, and answered questions from younger members representing a major part of the world across 50+ different countries.

In an organization like IEEE that has a global presence and major growth outside of the United States, you might expect to see and hear differences but what I saw were similarities. Aspirations to have a career in technology, impact change in the world, and grow personally. A universal spirit of optimism and cooperation was not just the norm, it was really the heart of the event.

The experience changed my perspective and opened my thinking to the opportunity that IEEE has to engage all over the world in common terms. There was no obvious division or boundary and it renewed a spirit for me. Multicultural night, where everyone dresses in the traditional clothing of their country and showcases their culture at a booth, was more about sharing than differentiating.

The values and mission of the IEEE organization can and do transcend geopolitical or other differences and that's a truly international experience.

Karen Bartleson, IEEE Past President

Countries in Story: South Korea and United States

A close colleague and fellow engineer invited me to visit South Korea. He was worried that I wouldn't have a pleasant experience, so he kindly sent me an email asking if I liked Korean food. I replied, "Korean food is delicious! The only thing I did not try when I was in Seoul a couple of years ago was live baby octopus. People with me put them in their mouths so the tentacles went into their mouths slowly. As we say in the US, 'Eww'." Clearly, I had no desire to try *that*!

When my colleague picked me up at the airport, he declared we would have live baby octopus for dinner so the tentacles could go slowly into my mouth. I laughed, knowing that he was teasing.

A group of us met for dinner, and someone announced that octopus was being served in my honor. People heard I did not get to try it on my previous visit. I was relieved, thinking it would be cooked. But they said, no, it would be alive because it's more expensive that way.

I was horribly trapped. Extra money and effort had been spent to give me a special dish as a show of respect. I could hardly decline and deeply insult my companions.

All eyes were on me as I touched the squirming octopus pieces with my chopsticks. As I picked one up, I was warned the suction cups could stick to the roof of my mouth! Mustering all my courage, I downed a few pieces and thanked everyone for their thoughtfulness.

If my email had said, "The only thing I do not want to try is live baby octopus", I would not have learned the lesson: communicate clearly, or eat the consequences.

Khaled Mokhtar, IEEE Senior Member

Countries in Story: Italy, Portugal, Egypt, USA and Brazil

I was 25 years old, packed with my engineering degree, lots of dreams, and hopes for a future that I never expected. At that time, I had lived my whole life in Cairo, Egypt where I was born and raised.

I got that opportunity to attend a huge Entrepreneurship Course in the University of California in Berkeley, Haas School of Business. At that time, I didn't even know how to pronounce the word: "Entre-Preneur-Ship".

I traveled alone, had my first experience in applying for a visa, booked a ticket via an agency (as electronic tickets were not so widely famous), and went to an airport "Departures" terminal. Every single tiny detail was engraved inside me, from Check-in, Security gates, Boarding, flight takeoff, Landing, Immigration office, and baggage claim! It was my first time ever trying use the internet on a flight, as it was a trial promotion on United Airlines. Naturally, I chatted with everyone I know using MSN Messenger.

I started to meet people from nationalities that I had only seen in football games; I never realized that Italians had a special, amazing kind of food, called "Italian", I never knew that Brazilians speak Portuguese, and I never knew that California belonged to Mexico in the past. I didn't imagine that I would go to sleep while my family back in Egypt were just starting their morning on the same day!

Internet was not that accessible from handheld devices at that time, so it took time for me to absorb all this information, and I decided to keep one thing with me from this experience: people.

That time, I realized the only thing that makes us who we are is having a network of amazing friends and family around us. I kept strong connections with people I met, used to send emails and keep in touch, and tried to meet again if the chance came.

Volunteering was in my blood; helping others and transferring the knowledge I have to those who may benefit from it was my passion. So, I decided to combine all my experiences with volunteering and started my journey in IEEE.

Since 2009, I have traveled to all the continents except for the frozen one. I made friends, brothers and sisters, connections, businesses, and a big, huge family that I never imagined would exist. My career path had changed dramatically, and my experience was shaped in a way that I never ever dreamt to have. That was not because of traveling by itself, but because of the people I met who shaped my life and made it totally different.

Maybe my story is too common for those who travel, but the uncommon thing that I can pass over through those lines is the **Art** of keeping people alive within our journey, the **Art** of making them part of our ride, and **the Art of seeing the World through the eyes of others**.

Qhansa Di'Ayu Putri Bayu, Telkom University Undergraduate Student

Country in Story: Sri Lanka

Meeting someone from overseas is like opening a new door to travel the world. My first time meeting foreign people directly was at IEEE R10 Congress 2015 in Sri Lanka. I couldn't believe that by joining an international event I could have new friends from other countries. So fun and great!

Rafal Sliz, IEEE Young Professionals Chair

Countries in Story: Poland, Finland, UK, Spain, Portugal, Germany, France, Czech Republic, Austria, The Netherlands, Belgium, Croatia, Bosnia and Herzegovina, Serbia, Sweden, Russia, Lithuania, Japan, Tunisia, Egypt, USA, Canada, Mexico, Costa Rica, Iceland, and Panama, Australia, and Ireland

Enable yourself.

Regardless of effort or organization, volunteering for me has never been a waste of time. I have always been involved in some activity, be it on a smaller or larger scale. Taking into account that I am an electrical engineer, IEEE was a natural choice.

After over a decade of volunteering for IEEE, I must admit that it has changed my perception of life, making it more complete and satisfying. It always comes at a price and the currency is time, the time we spend on making a difference. From my perspective, the most difficult part was to find a balance between my every-day life and volunteering. Since making a difference and interacting with people were always at the core of my existence, I often lose myself in volunteering. However, I have never been left empty-handed. The satisfaction of accomplishments is the greatest reward and that is all that I need. But IEEE gives more besides self-development; it creates an environment to promote and enhance your professional life.

Thanks to IEEE, I met people that I would never even imagine meeting, starting from world-leading technologists like Vinton Cerf, to celebrities like Grant Imahara from Mythbusters. Also, thanks to IEEE, I was able to work and tremendously advance my knowledge and experience in one of the best research groups in the world in the field of nanotechnology.

The benefits of volunteering are countless, but what I love most is people, who are so different, so full of energy and so motivated to change the world. Maybe it is trivial but having friends around the world makes you feel happier. IEEE provides a world eye-opening experience and the only question is: are you ready for it?

Robi Polikar, Professor and Department Head of Electrical and Computer Engineering

Country in Story: Japan

I planned – or so I thought – a meticulous itinerary for a day-trip starting in Tokyo through its suburb Hakone and ending in Kawaguchi ko, at the foot steps on Mount Fuji. There were many sites to see along the way, each connected with rail or ferry. What I had not known was that it was a holiday, and the schedules would end earlier. Only when I arrived at my last location did I realize the mistake.

In desperation, I went to the bus terminal, where the attendant was planning to leave at the end of his shift. He did not speak English, and well, I certainly did not speak Japanese. I showed him the map, pointing to Kawaguchi ko. He understood that I needed to get there by the end of the day. He looked at his watch, shook his head in disbelief, looked at his watch again, and then shook his head one more time. He pulled out a book of schedules, then another, and then another. He was trying to figure out something, and that something was not easy.

Then on a piece of Post-It note, he wrote down four names with what I understood to be bus stops, numbers, and times. He was routing me through four different locations. He put me on the first bus and gave instructions to the person sitting next to me. Thirty minutes later, that person told the driver to let me off, pointing me to another bus station across the street.

I waited there and when the bus came, I showed the driver my four-connection itinerary Post-It. After 10 minutes, he stopped and pointed me towards a shop next to the bus stop. I did not quite figure out why he wanted me to go to the shop, but that later became obvious. I went into the shop, not knowing what to say, other than to show the shopkeeper the original Post-It note.

To my astonishment, he walked out with me, closed his shop, and walked with me 10 minutes to another bus station. He waited with me for the bus to come and gave some instructions to the bus driver. That bus took me to the end of its line, at which point its driver walked me to the train station, where I would catch my last connection.

I did reach my destination that evening, but that would not have happened if it were not for the kindness of so many local people going out of their way to help me. Needless to say, I have a great respect and soft spot in my heart for Japan and its people.

Subodha Charles,
Researcher, Entrepreneur

Countries in Story: Sri Lanka, Australia, Indonesia, USA, France, Pakistan

A sunny end-of-winter day in Sydney. The rooftop cafe overlooking the circular quay is buzzing with people. Looks like everyone wants to grab a coffee in the cold weather. Sipping a cappuccino in a corner of the cafe, as I always love to do in any new city I am in, I am having some quality time to myself.

Coming from a tiny island in the heart of the Indian Ocean - Sri Lanka, I was lucky to travel quite a bit and live in different cities for extended periods of time. Visiting new countries and seeing famous tourist destinations is all good fun. Yet, nothing beats having a long walk in a strange new place, trying out local food, and chatting with the locals. That's when it hits you:

"Travel is such a fantastic self-development tool. It extricates you from the values of your culture and shows you that another society can live with entirely different values and still function and not hate themselves. It then forces you to reexamine what seems obvious in your own life and to consider that perhaps it's not necessarily the best way to live!" ~ Mark Manson

We live in our confined objective and imagined realities throughout our lives and accept things as they are. Yet, the moment you step out and immerse yourself in a different setup, your whole imagination expands. Parasailing in Nusa Dua, Bali, kayaking across the Hudson River, USA, listening to the choirs of Cathédrale Notre Dame de Paris, and taking a cross country trip on the top bunk of a train in Pakistan all made enormous contributions to my spirit. I'd prefer to spend on experiences over fancy gadgets because objects are expendable. Experiences are not!

Umair Mujtaba Qureshi, PhD Student, CS, City University of Hong Kong

Country in Story: Australia

My experience with IEEE had been like the politics of any third world country, i.e. "talk and do nothing". It all changed when I started my PhD in the Computer Science department at City University of Hong Kong (CityU HK) along with my wife Zunera Umair, who is also pursuing a PhD with me in the same department. After struggling for almost 2.5 years in my PhD journey, my life took a sudden turn with a change of supervisor. It was my new supervisor, Dr. Gerhard Petrus Hancke (Jr), with whom I had been working for the past 8 months.

In a month's time, Dr. G.P Hancke attended numerous conferences and academic visits, which made me curious about him. How did he manage to travel so much? Upon asking, he told me how he benefitted from IEEE meetups, and right there asked me to make a trip to Mid-Sweden University for a collaboration project. While staying in Sweden, we worked on two papers that were my first ever technical research papers during my PhD, which Dr. G.P Hancke asked me to submit to another conference held in Cairns, Australia. So from Sweden, my wife Zunera and I traveled to Cairns to attend the conference. Cairns was a wonderful town - the main attraction being the Great Barrier Reef.

The excitement began when both of my papers were accepted and I had some excellent reviews that boosted my confidence. Zunera and I were jumping out of the water: we booked a luxury apartment and enjoyed handsome halal meals. With this, I observed that if anyone has two papers or even one with good reviews, they should at least try for award competitions offered by the IEEE conferences. It simply makes your journey amazing.

I am positive, confident, and looking forward to submitting my work and enjoying more conferences, meeting new people, and making lots of amazing memories. I feel indebted to these conferences for all such experiences and those still to come.

Yu Wu, Data Scientist

Country in Story: United States

I have hosted more than 100 strangers from all over the world through Couchsurfing. We often spent a couple of days together, cooking dinners, walking around the neighborhood, checking out places I wanted to go but never went, and above all, having long conversations each other. Through these people and their stories, I feel like I am traveling the world in my small apartment. We become friends. Many of them went back to their countries and cities so far away yet still feel so close to my heart that I often think of them on any not-so-particular day. And those who stay in the area have become a part of my life. Some of them become my close friends, and so do so many people that I met through them.

I have changed tremendously in these years, and my couchsurfers are the ones I want to thank the most, for being so understanding, encouraging and inspiring, for helping me practice French and Italian, for participating in my photography project, for running beside me, for going to baseball games with me, for hosting me in their own countries, for introducing their friends to me, for showing me how much potential each and every one of us has if we dream big and try hard, for telling me being nice is appreciated, and being myself is the right way to go, for looking into my eyes, and without a single word, both of us know that our similarities overshadow differences, emotion transcends language, and humanity always prevails.

ABOUT THE AUTHORS

Jeffrey Eker Jr.

Atlanta – United States

 Jeff graduated from the Henry M. Rowan College of Engineering as an Electrical and Computer Engineering major and German Studies minor in 2016. He has traveled around the world in eight days, visited 23 countries outside of the US, and looks forward to visiting many more! Jeff is heavily involved with the Institute of Electrical and Electronics Engineers (IEEE), representing Young Professionals in the mid-Atlantic region of the US on the local and international level. Jeff has experience as a Technology Consultant and Portfolio Director of an innovation team.

Meeting people from around the world is always Jeff's favorite part of travel, and who he is today has been shaped in a huge way by the opportunities he's had to embrace local cultures. Jeff is the CEO and founder of Tediferous, LLC that created the CultureCloud® platform. The

CultureCloud mobile app allows travel users to instantly connect based on similar interests and hosts a community mode for any organization or conference to form a digital social ecosystem for their members. Jeff and his team launched CultureCloud at the 2016 Rio Olympics. He now also champions a project in Pakistan to crowd source opportunities for enabling social mobility in refugee populations.

Having grown up in Philadelphia, Jeff currently resides in Atlanta, GA and has been privileged to attend, moderate panels, and speak at many conferences globally including his TEDx talk in Bandung, Indonesia.

Sarang Shaikh

Karachi – Pakistan

Sarang Shaikh has a Telecommunications Engineering Degree and an entrepreneurial mindset with aspirations. He is developing expertise and specialization in ICT Program Management, Social Entrepreneurship, and Business Development. Currently, he is pursuing his

MBA in Entrepreneurship and Innovation and helping multiple universities in Pakistan to establish Innovation and Entrepreneurship Centers.

He has worked for two start-ups, accumulating a total of 8 years professional experience. He has also graduated with specializations in entrepreneurship from University of Maryland and IBA in Karachi. A student of life interested in Philosophy, Sarang is a strong believer of "Stoicism" and has published a book titled "Inspire your Motivations" available worldwide and is excited to publish *Living Globalized* as his second book.

With IEEE, he is Global Chair for IEEEmadC and has served in various positions ranging from a member of the Member Geographic Activities Training Committee, Public Visibility Committee, IEEE Infrastructure ad-hoc Committee, Asia-Pacific Humanitarian Activities Committee, and Senior Assistant Editor for the *IEEE IMPACT* Young Professionals Publication. He belongs to IEEE Karachi Section in Pakistan, where has been contributing his volunteer services for the past 9 years.

Made in the USA
Columbia, SC
13 February 2019